Kevin Le Moyne Cromley is the author of *Veering Off: My Search for Freedom*. He lives in San Diego, California, when he is not traipsing around the globe with his well-worn backpack and trusty pen.

To Laurel,
To fears being overcome
To adventures that lie in wait
For choosing a dram of serendipity
over a tankard full of fate…
to being the bravest person I know!

Kevin Le Moyne Cromley

DESVÍOS

A Memoir

AUSTIN MACAULEY PUBLISHERS™

LONDON * CAMBRIDGE * NEW YORK * SHARJAH

Ordering Information
Quantity sales: Special discounts are available on quantity purchases by corporations, associations, and others. For details, contact the publisher at the address below.

Publisher's Cataloging-in-Publication data
Cromley, Kevin Le Moyne
Desvíos

ISBN 9798886938890 (Paperback)
ISBN 9798886938906 (ePub e-book)

Library of Congress Control Number: 2023916309

www.austinmacauley.com/us

First Published 2024
Austin Macauley Publishers LLC
40 Wall Street, 33rd Floor, Suite 3302
New York, NY 10005
USA

mail-usa@austinmacauley.com
+1 (646) 5125767

Chapter 1

"Always treat women with respect." The words rattled inside my head as if on a loop, mixed with some godforsaken whooshing sound like rushing water or the churning of waves. A torturous cocktail forever grinding away inside my skull.

"Shut the fuck up, bitch!" The words shot from my mouth like bullets dipped in venom. Moments before I reached back and backhanded my wife of three months. I felt the smack of skin on skin, that weighty feeling when you know you've made a solid hit. It rattled through my van like a butcher tossing a slab of meat on a carving table. I waited for the return volley, the familiar pain of Mari's hand raining down atop my skull, loaded with her own venom-laced projectiles. But it never came, only the slamming of the van door as she retreated to our unhappy apartment.

I'd never hit a woman before. Ever. And I'd been smacked and clawed by plenty over my brief 29 years on this planet. No, I'd always stood there like a man and taken the abuse, relishing in my strength and fortitude to endure just such occasions. Because that's what real men do. They take the pain.

So, what had been the turning point tonight? How had I sunk to this pathetic new low? Was the screaming too loud, the tongue lashing too harsh? Were the blows to my head any harder than they had been in previous years, the pain too much to bear? Or had the shitpile of life—that toxic stew of bile and pus—risen so high that an explosion was as inevitable as magma ripping through the Earth's core?

What was it, exactly, that made me fall so far from my lofty perch? I'd always been taught to open doors for women and treat them with respect; to be caring and sensitive. To be a gentleman. At least that's what I thought I'd been taught. My mom had attempted to instill these traits in me, later in life, of course, after she'd sobered up. My father, missing in action—the quintessential 'deadbeat dad'—invariably absent from these life lessons.

Yet, regrettably, this boy—now man—possessed a deep well of memories. And, occasionally, those memories, and that pain—that sewage—spilled over and flowed like the Nile into my daily life.

* * *

"Where were you!" Mom screamed, rage in her eyes. I'd seen that fury so many times throughout my life. I kept my eyes trained on the floor, hoping her tirade would pass. She didn't need to know that I'd been inside my buddy Jim's garage smoking pot and blasting the new Mötley Crüe album, *Shout at the Devil.*

"I said where in the fuck were you, you little shit?" Her voice sank an octave deeper, that menacing tone when shit's about to get worse. Much worse.

But just as I was about to lower my head and resign myself to my fate, something happened. A shift. Mom's anger spread, rampaging about like a mutant virus. It leaped from her body into mine and traveled to every point in my body. My eyebrows furrowed, and my mouth hardened into a deep scowl. I was no longer a boy, I was rage. I was fury!

Mom stepped closer, face contorted, eyes black. "I said…where in the fuck were you?"

Time froze, icicles dangling from the minute hand, blood pumping through my aorta. Boom, Boom! Boom, Boom! Boom-Boom!

My biceps constricted into mounds of stone and my chest puffed out six inches. Then, through furrowed brow and squinted eyes, through rage and through fury, through a crumpled soul, I spit out those two magic words, "Fuck you!"

Her hand whipped across my face. *Whack!* I never saw it coming. My cheek was suddenly on fire, a red-hot iron pressed against it, my heart pulsating inside my lip. Mom stared into my eyes, searching for answers, waiting for my reaction.

I rubbed my tongue across my teeth, feeling the grit inside my mouth and liking it. I squeezed my eyes shut and snarled, "Do it again, bitch!"

The second smack came faster, and harder, spinning my head off its axis. My mouth filled with warm blood as I struggled to keep my balance and adjust to the darkness enveloping me. I was floating in space, orbiting the Earth and the Moon. I inhaled the emptiness, the peace.

Gravity returned, jolting me from my malaise. I lifted my head and stood as straight and as tall as I could, staring Mom dead center in the eyes. Then I grinned, "I said, do it again, you, fucking bitch!"

The third blow rattled my brain inside my skull. Molten lava now flowed down my cheek. A minute passed, then two, before I stood back up. Mom came into full focus, the devil incarnate. I swallowed the blood inside my mouth, thick and salty, as my throbbing lips formed the magic words once more. And there they sat, bullets chambered, ready to fire.

"You want another?" Mom asked in her smoky, violin-stringed voice.

I bit down on my lip. I was only thirteen, but strong as an ox. But what could I do? What could I possibly do? She was my mother. A female.

"I repeat. Do…you…want…another?"

I was silent for a moment, then shook my head no. I didn't want another. I didn't want any more pain. I just wanted to escape my life.

"That's what I thought," she said, before turning and walking away.

***

Now here I was, sixteen years later, having just smacked my wife across her face. And for what? Where was all that restraint and nobility now? A sudden fright raced through my body, eclipsing my need for answers. I patted my jean pockets. Left, right, left. Tapping my thighs as if they held the meaning of life. Searching, searching, searching. I felt the jagged outline of my keys and let out a sigh. I grabbed the rum bottle tucked snugly between my legs and drank down the last swallow. Liquid gold. Then I fired up my VW van and let out the brake. I still had ten minutes before the liquor store closed.

Chapter 2

Mari and I stood on a cliff overlooking the Pacific Ocean in Acapulco, Mexico, watching sleek and graceful divers hurl themselves into the ocean 100-feet below. Married just a week prior, an all-encompassing, true happiness enveloped me to my very core. Life was an unwritten book. An adventure lurking up ahead. I was on that upward trajectory I'd been searching for my entire life. I leaned in and whispered in her ear, "How 'bout we find a fancy hotel on the water and stay for a few days, then fly the rest of the way home?"

Mari's eyes widened. "But what about the big trip you wanted to take?" I could sense her worry. This was the first time she'd traveled outside of Nicaragua. The first time she'd been away from her family for any length of time. And I'd shoved her straight into the fire with my hardcore, backpacking, shoestring-budget expedition. We'd been traveling long and hard, and I could tell she was exhausted.

After saying our 'I do's' under the interwoven branches of avocado and mango trees, Mari and I left Nicaragua, setting off on a multi-country trek to the United States. We'd been traversing beautiful, yet rugged landscape ever since. But by the time we reached Acapulco, over a month later, we'd been attacked by every mosquito, flea, sandfly, and chigger in Central America. Our bodies were riddled with nasty bites, scabs, and welts. Even more disturbing, the incessant itching of our heads hinted more and more to the possibility— perhaps probability—we had lice. Staying in the cheapest of cheap hotels had taken its toll.

"But we don't have the money to fly home," Mari pleaded. "We…"

"Don't worry, we'll be fine," I assured her, before kissing her softly on the lips. The Peace Corps had given me a $4,000 readjustment allowance at the close of my service, and although I knew we'd need a good chunk of that to get an apartment once we finally made it to San Diego, I figured I'd get a job fairly quickly—what with having just saved Nicaragua and all. That and my trusty Chico State business degree promised a speedy slide back into gainful employment.

"Are you sure?" Mari asked softly, almost in a whisper, as if her voice might cause a landslide and hurl us into the sea below.

I looked out to the horizon. A powerful set of waves was barreling in. A sinewy man picked his way along the cliffs. Reaching a ledge, he dug his toes into the dirt. There he stood, facing the sea, poised and eager. I pulled Mari close, squeezing her tight as the waves smashed like freight trains against the cliffs. The tide was surging. Life progressing. With muscles flexed and arms spread wide, the man leaped into the air. Wind rushed across his body as he sailed down, graceful as a bird, and splashed into the waves.

Ever forward.

Chapter 3

"Look in the corners," I directed Mari, as we shoved our hands into the nooks and crannies of our shabby couch. A smile spread across her face as she pulled out her hand and opened her fingers, revealing a mound of quarters and dimes.

"Yes!"

Mari added the coins to the heaping pile of change we'd accumulated over the preceding hour. Life hadn't exactly moved *forward* since our arrival in San Diego. I was still searching for a job. Apparently 'saving Nicaragua' (or being a Returned Peace Corps Volunteer) didn't quite resonate on resumes or carry the heft I had assumed—perhaps hoped—it might. To make matters worse, we'd burned through most of the $4,000 putting a deposit down on our apartment and paying for rent and other living expenses; all leading to our current, unenviable situation, of scrounging through cushions and drawers in search of change to buy some food.

"*Solo dejame trabajar*—Just let me work," Mari repeated for what seemed like the millionth time. I'd heard that sentence, or variation of it, so many times I was hearing it in my sleep. And each time she asked, I gave the same reply:

"No, I want you to learn English. Go to your ESL classes and I will take care of us." I wasn't trying to be macho or anything like that; I just wanted her to learn English and assimilate into the American culture before being thrust into the workforce. She'd been working and struggling her entire life and deserved some time off to relax and enjoy life for a change.

Mari had been taking *English as a Second Language* classes since our arrival in the United States. She studied Monday through Friday, day and night, while I crisscrossed the breadth and width of San Diego, dropping off resumés, filling out job applications, and sitting through one nerve-wracking interview after another. And as our financial situation grew bleaker with each passing day, I dug in, undaunted, knowing that life would give me that bounce. Embracing the lessons that I'd learned while living in the magical land of

Nicaragua: to be strong and persevere; to battle on and never lose hope; to be true to yourself, in all ways, and at all times.

But our situation was now dire. The bounce had failed to appear, and I could no longer pay our rent or utilities. It was time to turn to the one person I'd been trying to distance myself from my entire life.

"Mom," I said sheepishly through the phone. "Can I come over? I need to talk to you."

She hesitated for a moment, a painful pause. "Sure, I'll see you in a bit."

The whooshing noise came roaring back as I drove, swirling inside my cranium like a whirlpool jet. Whoosh, whoosh, whoosh. I was in a tunnel, drums banging, fingernails rubbing against the grooves of a cello string. A guttural growl tickled my ear, harmonic in cadence, foreboding in measure.

Mom and I never talked about the shitty times. They were our little secrets now, buried inside dark caverns and bottomless pits. Our secret was that mom was an alcoholic when I was a kid. Vodka-her drink of choice. And when she got deep into the bottle, her demons were free to roam about, undisturbed, and unconstrained. And roam about they surely did. The slightest misstep: a broken plate, a raised voice—not being hidden from sight—all grounds for being lashed upon. All triggers for her smoky, melodic voice to morph into the deep, bestial growl which sent fear spiraling to every corner of my young body— knowing that her face would soon contort into a blood-red orb, with eyes ablaze and cigarette smoke trailing her every word.

"What do you got?" Mom asked, her words ricocheting through me.

What do you got? What…do…you…got? I flipped the words over in my mind. Each word, each syllable, like acrobats tumbling along a mat. What *did* I have, really? Besides an ego the size of Montana and some bullshit facade masking an ever-present fear of inadequacy. A belief that, perhaps, I just didn't measure up.

Was that *my* secret?

"I repeat, what do you got?" Mom's piercing green eyes stared into me, waiting for an answer, her gray hair pushed back over her ears. Her voice was soft, void of anger. The whooshing disappeared.

"I only have three hundred dollars and our rent is due on Thursday. I didn't know where else to turn."

She cupped her coffee mug in one hand and took a long drag on her Marlboro Red with the other. "How's the job hunt going?"

"Shitty, I've sent out over a hundred resumes and only had two interviews, but I think…"

"You need to take any job. Stop trying to get the best jobs out there."

"Well, I didn't go to college and spend two years in Nicaragua to get some shit job that barely pays the rent."

"Ha! Well, right now you can't even pay your rent."

She had me there. No fucking doubt about it. The easy slide I'd envisioned had failed to materialize. After two years in the Peace Corps, searching for some deeper purpose to my life, attempting to make sense of this complex world and where I fit in it, I'd returned to the U.S. and faced the possibility—perhaps probability—that I was just your average 'Joe Blow.' Another cog in the wheel. Nothing special. Nothing unique. Just another fucking number. Another fucking applicant.

"Look, I'm trying. You think I want to be here? You think this is easy for me? Standing here asking you for money?"

"No, I'm sure this is the last place on God's green earth you want to be right now. But here you are, nonetheless. Now how much do you need?"

"Shit, I don't know, maybe three or four hundred. I'll pay you back; I swear."

"Grab my purse on my dresser."

I stood and made my way to her bedroom. Mom still lived above my grandmother, who owned a four-unit apartment complex in University Heights, a quiet suburban area of San Diego. My sisters and I had lived here off and on over the previous two decades. It was a home base of sorts, between Mom's bouts of sobriety, when we'd travel from place to place and relative to relative.

I slid the purse across the table and watched as she pulled out her long, black wallet. "Now look, Kevin," she said, unsnapping the side button and pulling out a stack of 20s. Mom believed cash was king. In fact, I doubt she ever owned a credit card in her life. "Cash," she would always tell the cashiers when they asked, "Cash or credit?"

"Cash," she would tell the hairdresser at the beauty salon three blocks up, where women sat under astronaut helmets drying their red and yellow hair while I fidgeted in the beauty chair, embarrassed I was the only boy in America forced to have his hair cut and styled in a beauty salon. "Oh, what beautiful curls," the hairdresser would say while blowing cigarette smoke into the air and running her fingers through my hair. "What wouldn't I give for such beautiful loops?"

"Cash," I could almost hear her say as she slid the bills toward me. "I'm giving you seven hundred dollars. Notice, I said give, you don't need to pay me back. This is a wedding gift for you and Mari. But you'll have to make it last. I don't have the money to help you out again."

"Thanks, Mom…Thanks!" I said, leaping from my chair. "And don't worry, this is all I need. I'll have a job in a week. I just know it."

"Okay, sugar, I love you."

"I love you too, Mom." I couldn't run out of there quick enough, so excited I was to tell Mari that everything was going to be okay, that the upward trajectory—the bounce—was well within my grasp now.

But life can be a slippery fucker sometimes often leading us back to those dark caverns and bottomless pits, where the things we hold most dear, most precious, slip through our fingers while we're dancing with demons.

Chapter 4

The aroma of eggs on a hot skillet hit my nose as I cinched my tie and grabbed my suit jacket. I stared in the mirror, studying my reflection. It was time to begin my career. Time to show the world what a kid from the inner-city could do. Make a path, world, I'm coming through.

Mari handed me a plate of scrambled eggs, black beans, and a steaming-hot tortilla. She looked at me with a glow. Far different from that night in my van, weeks ago, when all the stress had reached a boiling point. The night I slapped her.

I suppose all roads had been leading to that point since the moment we departed Nicaragua following our wedding, traveling by bus through Honduras, El Salvador, Guatemala, and Mexico, attempting to eke out as much adventure as possible from our honeymoon. But traveling on the cheap will grind you down, even for a guy who'd just spent two years roughing it as a Peace Corps volunteer.

So, after a few days in Acapulco, relaxing and catching our breath, Mari and I flew the last leg of our journey home. After a bumpy flight to Tijuana, we flagged down a cab for the quick ride to the San Ysidro Border, a border I knew all too well, having crossed it hundreds of times as a kid, and later as a teen, to party into the wee hours of the morning along Tijuana's main drag, *La Revolución.*

When we reached the front of the pedestrian line, I handed the agent a sealed manilla envelope which the U.S. Embassy in Nicaragua had prepared for us. They escorted us into a small, plain office with dim fluorescent lighting to process Mari's paperwork. Another agent peppered us with questions, trying to determine if we had a fake marriage or not. "Why would you bring your new wife to the San Ysidro Port of Entry?" He asked, like I was some sort of scumbag for not flying her into San Diego.

I resented his question, at least, initially. But after looking around at the drab office and dirty floors, I saw his point. *Why hadn't we just flown into San Diego?* The simple answer: to save money. A hundred bucks to a Peace Corps Volunteer is all the money in the world. Being thrifty (cheap!) becomes second nature—a survival instinct. And for the last two years, that was all I'd known. Scraping by on two hundred bucks a month is no easy feat; $200 to cover your food, rent, utilities, travel…Beer!

"Welcome to the U.S.," the agent said, stamping Mari's passport with a dull thud. He led us through the building and past a long line of people waiting to cross, depositing us in front of a revolving glass door. Mari and I looked at each other briefly, then pushed our way through—into the awaiting arms of the good ol' U.S. of A.

It felt strange being home. Being back in my country after having been away for so long. I'd fantasized about this day forever, often while sharing a bottle of rum with fellow volunteers, quizzing each other about the first place we'd go upon our arrival. The answers invariably entailed food, and the different hamburger joints, steak houses, and Mexican restaurants we craved.

Perhaps *strange* wasn't the best word to describe how I felt. It was more a feeling of being disconnected, like walking into a stranger's home or meeting a relative you hadn't seen since childhood. I'd changed considerably over the past few years. Matured. No longer was I that wild and coarse boy from my youth. I was now a man.

Mari and I walked past a bright-red trolley and a sea of people rushing to unknown destinations. San Ysidro didn't look or feel much different from Tijuana, which added to my sense of disconnection. Further up the road, we stopped at a Jack-in-the-box parking lot. Mari moved closer, her eyes moving about, taking in the scene. There we stood, waiting, like prisoners on death row, for our ride. My younger sister, Kerry, arrived shortly after, in perhaps the biggest vehicle I'd ever seen: a Chevrolet Suburban.

"Oh, my god, it's so great to see you!" she said, before wrapping us up in bear hugs.

"This is Mari," I said proudly, a sparkle in my eyes. Mari's face turned red, a reticent smile struggling to emerge. Oh, what it must have been like for her. Arriving in an unfamiliar country. Meeting new people. Being unable to speak the language. I'd traveled that same path three years earlier. The day our 747 touched down on the Managua tarmac.

I put my arm around Mari and squeezed. *"Todo estará bien*—Everything's going to be okay," I assured her, as Kerry maneuvered onto the freeway. I marveled at the towering bridges and overpasses, the wide expanse of six-lane freeways and offramps that seemed to go on forever, staring in awe at the cement megastructures as we traveled north along Interstate 5. San Diego was so clean and modern. So grand in scale. Such a stark contrast from Nicaragua and all the Central American countries I'd grown accustomed to. For a moment, I almost didn't recognize my own country.

Kerry, excited about making us dinner, stopped at the local grocery store. She headed toward the meat section, while Mari and I wandered up and down the aisles staring at the endless array of food. Hundreds of jars of pickles and peanut butter. Frosted Flakes and Lucky Charms. Apple juice, mango juice, orange juice. Bananas and mangoes. Kiwi and watermelon. Asparagus and artichokes. Nearly every food known to man.

We spotted Kerry talking to the butcher. On either side, row upon row of freshly packaged meat—all neatly arranged and stored in clean refrigerator cases spanning from one side of the store to the other. He wrapped a soccer-ball-sized chunk of meat in a sheet of butcher paper and handed it to Kerry. I thought about how that one piece of meat could feed a small family for a month in Nicaragua. But I wasn't in Nicaragua anymore. I was in the U.S.

In the coming days, our senses would be inundated with a barrage of sights and sounds. Double-decker malls and fast-food joints. Stoplights and neon signs. Millions of cars and people all zipping through life in some freakish fast-forward mode. English, my native tongue, now seemed foreign as I struggled to find words. All these things I'd once seen and experienced, yet never questioned, these fabrics of my being, my identity—my very DNA—were now fractured and disjointed. I would have to relearn, reprogram. Plug back in. But one question hovered above the fog and confusion: Did I even still belong?

Toward the end of our Peace Corps service, nine volunteers from our original group of twelve attended a close-of-service workshop. The topic was on 'reverse culture shock,' a phenomenon known to affect people arriving home after living overseas for several years. Symptoms can include depression, confusion, restlessness, isolation. I remember thinking what an enormous waste of time it was, how none of these 'life lessons' applied to me. But now that I was back on my home turf—a strange, dystopian view of the world began cobbling itself together inside my brain. And from my vantage point—the outside looking in—I spied a society in chaos. Humanity without direction. People without purpose.

The shock didn't dissipate. In fact, if anything, it increased. I felt isolated and alone. Nobody understood me. Nobody shared my new outlook on life. Living abroad had peeled back my sheathing, leaving me bare and exposed. Stripped to my very core. My essence. Then, over time, it had reconstructed me. Turned me into something new. Something more. But nobody cared about these seismic changes swimming through my head.

I didn't tell Mari how I felt, at least initially, knowing she was finding her own way, navigating a strange culture and a new language. I talked to some of my old friends, who seemed genuinely interested in my experience, at least at first. But after ten or fifteen minutes, an icy sting hit me as I watched their eyes glaze over while retelling my transcendent Nicaraguan journey. Not that I could blame them. Hell, I'd once been them. Bored. Distracted. Uncomfortable.

To add to my litany of problems, I didn't *slide* right back into employment as predicted. I struggled to find a job, which only added to my stress. As a result, I drank. Even more than usual. Placing me quite squarely in the 'heavy drinker' category. Pre-Peace Corps, I'd been a mere 'beer drinker.' Post-Peace Corps, I'd added 'rum drinker' or 'rummy' as Hemmingway liked to call it, to my growing resumé. Rum being the perfect complement to my new, ever-burgeoning, apocalyptic-fuck-everything anthology on life.

When I ran out of friends to complain to, I turned to Mari. But she was having none of my self-indulgent, whiny-little-bitch views on life, growing weary of my penchant to pine on the 'good ol' Peace Corps days. As a result, we fought. Daily. "Stop complaining!" she'd demand, as I swirled my index finger through a glass of Bacardi and Coke while slumped over on our ratty couch. "This country has so much to offer, so many opportunities. Nicaragua isn't the great country you've built up in your drunk head. Just get a job."

"I'm fucking trying," I'd grumble, before taking another slug of booze in true 'rummy' fashion.

The shouting matches escalated, with Mari occasionally thumping me on my arm or my chest. A few smacks to the head to get my attention. To awaken me from my boo-hoo-poor-fuckin'-me pity party.

"Ahh, just fuck off," became my go-to response, my mantra, followed by a wobbly search for the keys and a dash out the door. *Can't a guy just drink in peace?*

We were heading down a dark road. And fast. All culminating that night in my van. The night we ran out of pavement. The night I smacked Mari.

"You need to quit drinking!" Mari screamed, sliding the van door open and crawling in the back. Scaring the shit out of me in the process. She must've followed me out of the apartment in stealth mode, I thought, while reaching for my bottle of rum.

"Get out!" I demanded, pointing to the sliding door.

"I'm not going anywhere. You're too drunk to drive. If you want to kill yourself, you're going to have to kill me, too."

"Oh, stop being so melo-fucking-dramatic and get the fuck out already."

That's when I felt the thump on my head. The same whack Mom had delivered years before. The same sting, the same pain—the same molten lava dripping down my neck. Then came another and another and another. Finally, I'd had enough. Enough pain. Enough frustration. Enough incoming fire. I'd just had enough, plain and fucking simple.

I didn't realize it then, but that moment was a turning point. What I did grasp, however, was that I'd sunk to an epic new low. Lost that part inside me that made me who I was. That made me unique. Yes, on that dark night, where all roads ended, and the music reached its crescendo, I'd become what I'd always feared: Ordinary.

A few years earlier, I'd had an 'awakening' while running around a bonfire in El Socorro, Mexico. A flash of light. A voice. A feeling. The universe had reached out and grabbed me. Ripping me from my known orbit and fixing me on a new and unchartered trajectory. A trajectory that led me to join the Peace Corps and move to Nicaragua where I met a stranger who taught me the importance of looking inside, of prowling the corners of my soul and meeting the boy residing within. This same stranger taught me how to view the world in a new way, to filter out the bullshit we're taught from day one, to differentiate between perceived importance and profound importance.

But now that I'd returned from far-away lands, I found myself tumbling. Veering from those foundational paths—losing myself in the jungles once more. It was imperative I talk to this stranger again. Before I'd strayed too far. Before it became too late.

Mari and I had a long talk the following day. I told her I could never go through that again—that *we* could never go through that again. Our relationship had become too volatile. And if she ever hit me again, or me her, it would be the end of us. We'd reached critical mass, and any further steps along that path would lead to a nuclear explosion.

Mari moved her head closer to mine, her eyes puffy and exhausted. "Stop drinking, Kevin, you're killing yourself." Pleading words. Dire words. My heart sank. I had to get my shit together.

Chapter 5

Finally, after a two-month stint on the Great American Job Hunt, I landed a job in finance. I'd be selling mortgage loans to purchasers of manufactured homes and plots of land to place them on. The position entailed extensive travel throughout California, Arizona, New Mexico, Nevada and Utah where I'd meet with mortgage brokers, mobile home park owners, and sales agents, convincing them to finance their loans through our bank.

I would spend the first two weeks in the office, training, before hitting the road. A wave of happiness rolled over me; excited by this amazing opportunity and the sense of freedom that came with travel. I wouldn't be chained to a desk or work the traditional nine-to-five grind. I wouldn't have to fight traffic while commuting to an office each day. No, I would travel the open road-making my own schedule, being my own man. The perfect job for a guy who'd spent the last two years swinging in a hammock.

Convincing Mari was tough. She was thrilled, of course, that I'd found a job. And a decent job at that. But she was less enthused about all the time I'd be away from home, traveling for weeks at a time. We'd been closer than ever since 'the talk.' I'd even cut back on my drinking, returning to 'beer-drinker' Kev, and only on weekends. I knew I couldn't fully lick it. But I'd at least attempt to control it. Put it back in its box. Order within chaos.

I devised a three-step plan to get my shit in order. Fuck the twelve-steps, I was taking the abridged version. The CliffsNotes Course.

Step 1: Get a job. Check!
Step 2: Relax the mind.
Step 3: Quit drinking.

So, while Mari was away at ESL classes, I checked out a few books on Buddhism, hoping to find that ever-elusive balance. Zen Buddhism especially piqued my interest, as it wasn't so much a religion as a way of life. A philosophy. Some call it a journey. I drew parallels to my own life: clearing your mind of the known, breaking free from authority, searching for peace.

The destination of all Buddhists is self-enlightenment. To truly know oneself. To reach a state of being that is at once everything, yet nothing: Zen.

Monks in Kyoto, Japan sit perfectly still for hours each day, their hands folded in their laps, not making a sound. The head monk ensures nobody falls asleep by lightly tapping the shoulders of any nappers with a bamboo rod known as the 'Zen Stick.' These monks dedicate their entire lives to the practice of Zazen. Sitting in silence, clearing their mind, seeking enlightenment. Searching for Zen.

Life hadn't exactly lined my path with rose petals. Often bloodied and bruised along the way. But maybe, just maybe, if I played my cards right, I might find a slice of that Zen.

Pulling into the parking lot for my first day of work, my stomach was full of butterflies. I was nervous, but eager to begin my career. The glass building was modern and classy, and once inside, they directed me to Human Resources, where I filled out the customary new-employee forms. I smiled when checking the 'married' box for the first time in my life. Another man, older with curly hair and a thick mustache, took a seat next to me. "Hey, there," he said, "looks like we're the newbies."

"Appears that way," I replied. "You think they have enough forms?"

"Typical bank," he laughed. "Forms, forms, forms."

His name was Phil, and he was a fellow sales rep. I raced through the forms and handed them back to the Human Resource lady, ready to begin my corporate adventure. Perhaps all the books on Buddhism were having their desired effect, because I no longer equated having a traditional job or career with a death sentence. It wouldn't be the end of the world. And I could exist, perhaps even thrive, in this new realm. Besides, this was still my country and my culture, after all.

Phil and I shot the shit while waiting in the conference room. He was from Northern California and had spent over twenty years as a traveling sales agent. My mind wandered, wondering if Phil represented my future, when a thin man with salt-and-pepper hair and a neatly trimmed goatee came in and shook our hands. "Welcome, gentlemen, I'm Jim, Vice President of our Western Division. It's good to meet you both. Phil, would you please follow me back to my office?" Phil grimaced, as if he'd been summoned to the principal's office.

"Good luck," I said as he followed Jim down the hall.

I took a moment to survey my surroundings. Everything was glass and wood, wood and glass, and flowed seamlessly and elegantly together. It was official: I was back in the working class. Had the last two years of my life really existed? If so, what did 'joining the corporate world' say about me now? Was I selling out? Turning away from all I'd discovered in Nicaragua? A traitor to my newly formed transcendent spirit? Or was that all just a crock of shit?

The HR woman introduced me to Jenny, a small and energetic young lady who'd be training me for the day. "Hi, welcome to the Western Division. Follow me and we'll get started." We moved swiftly through the office, with Jenny pointing out the various break rooms and copy rooms, the bathrooms and executive lounges, all while waving and greeting people as we made our way to a back section of the building where the corridors narrowed, and the windows trickled away. Was I entering George Orwell's Ministry of Truth?

After passing through a final hallway, we entered a large wing brimming with computers, cubicles, and desks, twisting through the room like a futuristic electronic snake. Every open space was crammed with bodies staring mindlessly into monitors. Fluorescent lights flickered overhead, and a steady hum hung heavy in the air. I'd entered the belly of the beast.

"Sit here," Jenny said, snapping me out of the dark trance I found myself sliding into. She pointed to an open cubicle and chair. "I'm going to teach you how we input loan applications into our software program today."

"Ok," I replied with a fake smile, wondering how in the fuck I could escape this grim, 1984 dystopian novel I'd stepped into. Perhaps, I wasn't just your stereotypical, whiny alcoholic complaining about the constraints of modern-day life, after all. Or, more probably, I *was* a stereotypical, whiny alcoholic, yet my assessment of modern-day life was spot on. Either way, I needed to learn the basics of this mortgage business, *quick*, so I could get on the road and out of this nightmare.

Jenny grabbed a stack of loans from a communal pile that rose three-feet high. "This is our loan application." She taught me how to enter the relevant information into the computer system. I glanced around from time to time as she typed, staring at all the pod people diligently tapping away on their keyboards as a row of fax machines chirped away behind us, loan applications rolling off them like candies in a candy factory.

Jenny tapped my arm to get my attention. "After you've entered all the applicant's information, hit this button here to print the forms. Then place them in the underwriter's box next to the fax machines."

"Where does the loan go from there?" I asked. Jenny appeared confused, as if that question had never been posed to her before.

"Well, I suppose it goes to the underwriter for approval," she finally said.

"Or denial," I quickly added.

Jenny didn't respond, just grabbed a stack of applications and dropped them on my new desk. "Start with these and I'll check back with you in a few hours." She disappeared into a maze of cubicles as I stared blankly at the stack of papers, gears grinding loudly inside my head. I grabbed the top sheet off the pile and banged away on my keyboard, fingers blazing, blocking out the clatter from my fellow pods.

By noon, I had the software dialed in and was knocking out loans every ten minutes. I wanted to prove to the company what a wise decision they had made by bringing me onboard. That I was a team player and willing to work hard. A valuable asset.

"So, how did you do?" Jenny asked, pulling me out of my virtual coma.

"Not bad, I guess. I've entered in twenty so far."

"Twenty? You've entered in twenty applications already? Whoa, slow down, you're going to make us all look bad. We average twenty applications a day."

"Oh, sorry," I replied with a nervous smile. "Well, this is all temporary, anyway. I'm just learning the different operations of each department before I move on to sales…So, what are we training on after lunch?"

"Sales? Hmm, I don't know anything about that. I'm just training you in data entry."

The gears ground even louder as Jenny walked away, leaving me alone in my sad little cubicle. I felt the Zen Stick on my shoulder. And not a gentle stroke to wake me from a peaceful nap. But a ferocious blow that dug into my muscle and my psyche. My body constricted. Something was off. Something out of balance…

Something not Zen.

Chapter 6

It was dark by the time I raced up the stairs to our second-floor apartment, the night having long since cast its shadow over San Diego. Day one of my re-entry into the *real world* was officially complete, accompanied by a mounting sense of dread for the thousands more that lay ahead. But I took solace knowing that once I finished training, I'd be out of the office and free once again.

The sweet smell of sizzling meat greeted me as I threw my tie on a chair and hugged Mari from behind, brushing my cheek softly against hers. She smiled and continued to stir onions and potatoes around a pork roast. Everything seemed right—so adult and mature. Who knows, maybe this could work out. I grabbed a beer from the fridge and plopped down in a chair. "How were your English classes?"

"Bien." She continued to brown the onions.

"Talk to me in English!"

"*No, me da pena*-I'm embarrassed."

"Oh, come on, how are you supposed to learn English if you never speak it?" I drank the last of my beer and grabbed another.

"*Después*-later." She cut off a chunk of pork and put it on a plate, adding a heap of red beans and draping a tortilla over the top. "*Aquí.*" She handed me the plate, then made one for herself.

I slid off my shoes. "So, how was the rest of your day?"

"Good. I cleaned the house and organized our clothes. I tried using the vacuum, but it was too hard. So, I swept instead."

"Wait...you swept the carpet?"

"Yes."

I tore off a piece of tortilla and used it to scoop up a mixture of pork and beans. "You know they invented the vacuum to make life easier, not harder."

"Well, it's a stupid machine." A flash of anger lit up her eyes like fireworks. "Besides, it's probably broken, anyway."

I held back a chuckle, washing down my food with a swig of beer, each drop like a burst of life, a resurrection of my spirit. "Hold on." I stood and trotted off toward the closet, returning with the cheapo Eureka we'd paid twenty bucks for at the Goodwill. "Now show me what's so hard about it."

Mari's face was still red. She had so much pride. So much grace. She snatched the vacuum from my hands, plugged it in, and hit the power button. Then, gripping it in both hands, like a baseball player holding a bat, she pushed the vacuum around the living room in its upright position, straddling it awkwardly between her legs. My face turned as red as hers as I tried desperately to hold back a smile. But after a few minutes, my body gave in, and I erupted in laughter. I laughed so hard my sides ached, forcing me to bend over and take in deep breaths as I tried to control myself.

Mari, now beet red, turned off the machine. "What's so funny? Stop laughing!" I laid on the carpet and held my belly, trying not to pee myself.

"What's wrong with you? Stop it! Stop it!"

"I'm sorry, I'm sorry," I cried through bursts of laughter and gasps of air, tears rolling down the corners of my eyes. I eventually gained some control and stood back up. "Here," I said, through bursts of laughter, grabbing the handle of the vacuum and depressing the lever near the base with my foot. "See," I gasped, "you just tap this button here to unlock it, then you can push it around easily."

She stared at the vacuum for a moment. Then her eyes widened, and a sunrise spread across her face. "Oh, my god, how embarrassing!"

I don't think I could have loved her any more than I did then.

***

Friday rolled around, and I was still entering loan applications into the system—and growing angrier by the minute. There had been zero meetings about the sales position they had hired me for. Or training in any other aspects of the business. Adding to my sense of unease, Phil, the guy I'd met on my first day—the other sales rep—seemed to be MIA. Where was he? Why wasn't he training in data entry like me?

I stared at my computer screen. Applicant: Ralph Stevenson. Current Employer: Taco Bell. Job Title: Assistant Manager. Loan requested: $280,000. Are you fucking kidding me? I'd come to realize that 90% of the applicants didn't deserve a credit card, much less a mortgage loan. Here I was still driving a beat-up, 1972 VW van, positive I couldn't swing a car loan, and this chump wants $280,000?

I tugged at my collar, my neck itchy and hot. My tie felt like a noose cinching tighter by the minute. My blood boiled when I spotted VP Jim floating through the office. There was something about his light-gray suit—the creased slacks, narrowed at the ankles and slim-fitting jacket—that made me want to throw him out of one of the plate-glass windows.

They'd even come up with a term for guys like him since I'd been away: 'metrosexual.' Not that he was overly effeminate. In fact, he was married with kids. But he was just too damn slick. Maybe that's what pissed me off the most about him. That he chose to dress this way. Chose to act this way. He was a scalpel, while I was a dull blade. He glided through the office, a leopard hunting prey, while I lumbered about, a bull looking for a clump of grass— talking too loudly and wearing oversized, blue suits I'd scavenged from the Salvation Army.

Perhaps I was just pissed off because this was day five and I was still doing data entry without the slightest hint of training in other areas; or word one when I'd be setting out on my much anticipated 'open road.' Maybe that's why, when I saw him breezing through the office that morning, I knew it was time for a confrontation. Knew it was time to let VP Jim know I wasn't some little bitch content to sit quietly by in my little prison cubicle for the rest of my life. Besides, if I had to enter one more idiot into the computer for a loan, they were utterly unqualified for, I'd be taking a Zen Stick to every motherfucker in that office, an act I'm quite certain Buddha would disapprove of.

Blood rushed through my aorta as I steamed toward his office. *This is it. I'm not playing this charade any longer.* I burst in without a knock, ready for war. But before I could utter a single word, my eyes were transfixed— mesmerized—by the lush green golf course sitting just outside his window. *Fucker!* Jim's head popped up from his laptop, his eyes registering alarm.

"Jim," I grumbled in my deepest voice, holding back the dam of rage welling up inside. "I'm supposed to be a sales agent, but all I've done this entire week is data input. What is going on?"

He rolled back in his big black executive chair as I inched closer, his eyes widening with my every step. Now, *I* was the hunter, ready to pounce, yet my gaze kept shifting from my prey's salt-and-pepper hair and perfectly trimmed beard to the rolling green hills and flowering trees of the valley below. No longer did I want to toss Jim through his floor-to-ceiling window but jump through it myself. Freedom lay just beyond that glass, and oh how it beckoned.

"Kevin," Jim said, breaking the spell of life beyond our glass prison. And the illusion of running through the grass with arms out wide. "We're going to train you in the different aspects of the business. But first we have to…" He droned on, eyes darting from a fluorescent light above my head to a picture of a sailboat on a wall to my side.

He looked everywhere except in my eyes, making shit up on the fly. A bullshitter can spot a fellow bullshitter from a mile away, and I was most definitely being served up a heaping pile of crap! I shifted my weight from one foot to the other. My toes, crammed into pointy leather wingtips, felt like kidnap victims stuffed inside a trunk. The word 'Vision' was written above the sailboat. I squinted, attempting to read the quote underneath as Jim rambled on, his voice like a dull drill bit pressed against my skull.

"Oh, come on, man," I finally said, interrupting him mid-speech. "I picked up your data entry system in the first fifteen minutes I was here. It needs a complete overhaul, by the way." Then, putting my own bullshitting methods to use, I bluffed, "And I know Phil is already in the field. What area is he working? Wait, don't tell me…mine."

Jim's eyes came to a stop, their schizophrenic flight having landed on yours truly. He stared with questioning eyes. I returned his stare, peering straight through his cornea and into his cerebral cortex. The engine was cranking up, and that distant clicking in his brain meant that he'd made the discovery: I wasn't the Neanderthal I often appeared to be. That my brooding eyes and broad shoulders were not signs of a deficient intelligence, but characteristics of genetic evolution. Of progress. At least that's what I liked to tell myself.

Jim leaned back in his chair. "Ok, I'll be straight with you. There was a mix-up. We hired two sales reps for the same position. Phil did take your region. We'll put you in the field at the next opening."

I muttered 'fuck' under my breath, wondering if my primitive biceps could toss him and his fancy leather chair out the window in one fell swoop. I took a deep breath in and exhaled slowly. I'd suspected something was off but hearing it out loud was a punch to the gut. I ran my fingers through my scalp and grunted, "And when will that be?"

"Listen, this is all coming from above me. I wasn't even involved in the hiring process."

I stared out the window to the green valley below, imagining myself rolling down the hill on my side as I did when I was a kid. As I did when I was free.

"Listen, just finish out today in loan input and I'll put you in a new position on Monday. We'll rotate you through the different positions until a sales area opens up."

"Like I said," I repeated, still staring out the window, "when will that be?"

Jim swiveled in his chair, following my gaze to the green paradise below, both of us wishing our worlds existed there. But they didn't. They existed here. In the glass and wood world of finance. "Six months to a year," he finally said.

My salivary glands kicked into overdrive. All I could think about was rushing outside and drinking a beer. I could almost taste it flowing down my throat.

"Fine," I said.

Walking away, I remembered the sailboat on the wall. She was listing to port, sails taut, cruising into the sunset. 'Vision,' it read, 'the art of seeing what is invisible to others-Jonathan Swift.'

I went back to my cubicle and stared at the blinking cursor.

Chapter 7

Falling in love for the first time is a poignant moment in a boy's life. Mine came in the fifth grade. And oh, what a ride it was. Better than any rollercoaster in the world. When gravity fades and the impossible becomes possible. When one needs but to stretch out his arm to touch the moon or to flick a star. Yes, within that moment, we become immortal. Walking on clouds. Peering into solar systems. The moment when the world, and all within it, becomes our own.

Yet love, as we come to learn in time, can be a treacherous thing. That which appears to be true can just as easily be untrue. Romeo, brokenhearted at the sight of his beloved Juliet's lifeless body, puts poison to lips and drinks away his pain. Yet Juliet was not dead. And upon waking, and seeing her Romeo no more, plunged a sword into her breast. Such can be with love…

Carla Cameron was the prettiest girl in John Adams Elementary. With dirty-blonde hair and amber eyes that sparkled in the sun like splotches of honey. She was skinny and short, much like me, and wore skintight Jordache jeans and flowery OP shirts. And when she sprinted across the blacktop, with the fuzzy balls at the back of her socks bouncing up and down against her blue-and-white checkered Vans, my heart raced right alongside her.

But before Cupid could draw his bead upon my chest, I met a friend. A fellow traveler who was curious and like-minded. Over time, he'd teach me the virtue of patience, and the merits of seeking new and more interesting paths. As a result, I'd become less jaded, less cynical about the world around me. Trophies I'd carry with me throughout my life.

I was new to the rough-and-tumble, blue-collar neighborhood of Normal Heights in central San Diego. Mom, smart as a whip, had miraculously sobered up. Having previously concluded that drunken benders superseded her duty to parent. A determination that led to years of heartache for my sisters and I. Longing for her touch. Her embrace. Her affection. Her love…

My sisters and I were back in her custody. All living together in a two-bedroom house in an alley behind Adams Avenue. And just in time for my entrance into the fifth grade. But the lighthouse was flashing warning signals. Danger lurking just beyond the horizon.

Entering Ms Baley's fifth grade class was a nerve-wracking proposition that first day. I'd already had to navigate the half-mile walk down busy Adams Avenue with my little sister, Kerry, as my sole companion. Coming face-to-face with kids of all different colors and cultures was a complete one-eighty from the rural, lily-white town of Santee, where I'd lived previously with a mostly absent father and a stepmother from hell.

I took a seat next to a skinny kid with a goofy smile and a mop of straight-blonde hair. Hair so blonde it appeared white. After introducing ourselves, I thought he was pulling my leg. "Hey, man," I asked with a tilt of my head. "What's your name again?"

"Trout," he repeated, his smile now a half-grin, half-smirk which told me he was probably telling the truth, forced to repeat it a million times in the past. Before I could say anything witty, or 'fishy,' his smile returned, and he added, "Well, to be perfectly honest, my full name is Justin Cody Trout Fishing in America Rogers."

"Yeah right!" I said, "And I'm King Kong, ruler of the Amazon Jungle."

"Well, nice to meet you, Kong, because that really is my name. Justin Cody Trout Fishing in America Rogers." His big, goofy grin returned. "But you can just call me Trout."

"Wow, really?"

"Yes, really, my mom named me after some song or book from the 60s. She was a hippie."

"Radical, man." I made the peace sign with my fingers. "Hey, you want to go to the arcade after school?"

Trout flashed his own peace sign. "Sounds groovy."

And that's how our friendship began; two boys eager to explore life, to share the secrets amassed over a turbulent ten years on this Earth. We'd be joined at the hips for years to come, experiencing many firsts along the way: kissing a girl, copping a feel, smoking a joint.

Trout's mom, Jessica, worked as a sales agent for the Hyatt Islandia, a high-rise hotel on Mission Bay. Occasionally, she'd let us tag along with her to the hotel. And while she was busy wining and dining NFL coaches and general managers from visiting teams, Trout and I tore through the hotel like hooligans on the prowl. Sprinting past the pool and clubhouse, through the gym and lobby, and into the elevator for the quick ride up to our favorite spot on the property: the 18th floor Penthouse, where, if it hadn't been rented for the evening, we were free to lounge around on the couches like big shots, ordering room service and watching TV.

When we grew bored with Tom and Jerry, we raced out to the observation deck, staring out at the city lights, dazzled by their shimmer and brilliance. A million lights dancing across Mission Bay, illuminating the sailboats as they rocked gently in her palm.

"Bet I can chuck this into the water," Trout said, holding an unopened can of Coke into the air. Before I could respond, he turned and hurled it into the sky. It spun through the air, flipping end over end in a perfect arc, before exploding on the sidewalk eighteen stories below.

We instinctively ducked, crawling like army men under razor wire to the safety of the suite. "Dude, are you insane!" I barked, my adrenaline spiking. As we lay there hunkered down, waiting for hotel security, or worse, the cops to ring the buzzer, Trout leaned in and whispered, "Your turn."

After ten minutes, we determined the coast was clear and poked our heads up. Not wanting to be outdone, I dug around the mini fridge, pulling out a handful of Coke and 7-Up cans. With sinister grins, we tiptoed back to the railing. "Look out below!" I hollered, chucking the green can into the air.

Jessica, or Jess to her friends, had a zeal for life that was unmatched. Being a single mom in a male-dominated profession didn't slow her down in the least. Once a devout hippie, she clung to her bohemian, free-bird roots, while simultaneously kicking ass in the modern world. One foot planted in each world.

My love for travel and exploration came courtesy of Jess who, when the urge to break free arose, headed straight for Mexico—with Trout and me in tow. We'd swim all day at the Rosarito Beach Hotel, sun blazing down on our skin, while Jess cracked sunflower seeds and scribbled in her journal at the pool's edge. When the sun dipped, we drove to the small fishing village of Puerto Nuevo and ordered rounds of lobster. She showed me how to pile chunks of sweet lobster on a tortilla, add a scoop of beans and rice, then dip the whole thing into a bowl of warm, melted butter.

After dinner, while Jess sipped ice-cold Tecates and joked with the servers, Trout and I wandered along the cliffs out front. Then, just before sunset, we raced down to the shore and collected colorful shells and pebbles, waves crashing at our feet and birds screaming and carrying on, diving into the water repeatedly. The sky began its metamorphosis, its blue hues changing from yellow to orange, before exploding into a medley of red and purple as the sun slipped below the horizon. Jess's freedom—her verve for life—seeping into our DNA with each step we took in the wet sand. Our footprints, a testament to the life we would one day live.

On Friday nights, the three of us headed to Tuba Man's, a bar in North Park, one neighborhood over from Normal Heights. Because they served food, albeit bar food, Trout and I were allowed inside—some kind of legal loophole. We were to stay clear of the main bar area, but of course we never did. And nobody seemed to care. Jess was a regular, and now, so was I.

Nearly every square inch of the walls and ceiling were covered in sports memorabilia and odd trinkets: bicycles, horns, road signs, dollar bills, musical instruments, and a host of other strange items. One wall was dedicated to San Diego sports teams, with autographed pictures of Padres and Chargers players. A giant golden tuba, prominently displayed in a glass case near the entrance, greeted each customer. 'Tuba Man' was an actual person, who played his golden tuba for scores of adoring fans at San Diego Padres games.

"We need more quarters," I told Trout. Jess had been feeding us a steady stream of coins throughout the night, but we felt bad returning to her end of the bar every twenty minutes, like beggars.

"Let's look around the bar," Trout said before crouching into stealth mode and crawling around the barstools. I followed him around the bar, tapping my hand along the sticky carpet and scooping up quarters and dimes that had fallen out of the pockets of drunks. We were invisible to the people laughing and shouting just above us.

When we'd found enough change to keep us occupied, we ran back to the gaming area to play Space Invaders and pinball. Jess's laughter rang out across the bar as she drank beer from a frosted mug and flirted with a guy with a scruffy beard. When we ran out of coins, he was more than eager to feed us a steady diet of quarters to keep us away.

Growing bored with pinball, we roamed through the smoky bar on secret missions: stealing matches off the bar top, sneaking pizza sandwiches from the pickup counter, tickling women's legs as we crawled under their bar stools. Upon completion of each mission, we followed Jessica's laughter back to home base.

We soon grew bored with the bar as well and snuck out. Back in secret stealth mode, we ran up University Avenue on a top-secret spy mission to save the world. The stars lit our way, carrying us into the wee hours of the night. Trout sprinted into the villain's hideout, a 24-hour laundromat. Unable to find the assassin, we changed tactics, attempting to smoke him out. We stuffed napkins into a wood-paneled mail slot, then reached into our pockets and pulled out the matches we'd swiped off the bar. I lit one of mine, then Trout lit his.

"You first," he said.

I didn't hesitate, just tossed the lit match into the slot. Trout quickly followed, dropping his match into the chute. "We'll smoke that bastard out," he said. A puff of gray smoke rose out of the mail slot, followed by the crackling of burning paper. Our eyes doubled in size, petrified, when the smoke turned black and stank.

"Dude," I said, shaking Trout. He stared blankly at the black smoke pouring from the opening, the wood paneling now streaked with soot. A flame shot out of the mail slot, its bright-orange tail slapping against the wall. The crack, like a lion tamer's whip, sent Trout and me sprinting back to Tuba Man's.

"Water, water, give us water. Lots of water," we shouted to the bartender. He lined up several glasses. "Okay, okay, just settle down. Here's your water. Now, go have fun on your little adventures."

We sprinted to the laundromat at top speed and dumped the water into the slot. Gray smoke billowed up, but moments later the flames returned, red-hot claws scraping across the wood. "We need more water!" Trout screamed, grabbing my shirt and dragging me out the door.

We raced to the bar for a second round of waters, then back to the laundromat. Pouring the water in slow and steady, like trained firefighters, focusing our aim and working as a team. Black smoke spewed from the mail slot, followed by the stench of soggy, burned wood and paper. The fire was out.

"Let's get the fuck out of here!" I screamed. Trout and I took off, running as fast as our legs would carry us back to Tuba Man's. We sprinted past the golden tuba and the autographed wall. Slipped by Jess, still laughing and carrying on with the bearded guy, oblivious to our brush with arson. Then jumped back on the pinball machine as if nothing had ever happened as if we hadn't almost just burned down the laundromat up the block. We were secret agents, after all. Our work, classified. Saving the world didn't come with recognition. But today, evil had been defeated.

Mission complete.

Chapter 8

VP Jim was true to his word, and I spent the next few months learning the ins and outs of the finance business. From debt-to-income ratios and discount points to compound interest and APR. I buried myself in the numbers, absorbing the intricacies and nuances of underwriting and funding loans.

And fund loans we surely did with a fervor that grew exponentially with each passing day. Loan after loan, like an itch that can't be scratched. The pace was frenzied and untenable. Yet we continued on, our bank morphing into Dracula, sucking blood from unsuspecting victims which turned out to be anybody with a job and a credit score. *Any* credit score. *Anybody* with a pulse, really.

Dracula's thirst was insatiable, needing a constant supply of fresh blood. Fresh blood and fresh applicants. Shockingly, the collection department's ranks swelled. Everybody feigning ignorance about the correlation between loans funded and loans defaulted. A symbiotic relationship, despite neither department ever speaking to the other as if we were separate, independent companies, indifferent to the plight of the other. When in reality, we were all passengers on the same ship, all subject to the same laws of physics.

One morning, after seeing a post-it note that read "Approve this one!" scrawled in Jim's handwriting, on a loan I'd rejected just the day prior because of the guy's shitty credit record and the fact that he only made $9 an hour cleaning windows, I'd had enough.

Into Jim's office I barged, application held high in the air, righteousness streaming off it like a banner in a storm. "There's no way I'm approving this fucking guy!"

"What?" Jim peeked up from the stack of files and papers spread helter-skelter across his desk. My guy—my applicant—was just another blip on the radar, another grain of sand on an endless beach.

"The window washer guy. His credit sucks. He has three 90-plus and six 30-plus over the last three years." Underwriter jargon for past due accounts on his credit report.

"Yeah, but isn't he current now? Nothing within the last ninety days?"

"Jim…he makes $9 an hour. How's he going to swing a two-hundred-and-fifty-thousand-dollar loan payment?"

"Do we have a co-signer?"

And there it was, the secret to making any pile-of-shit loan smell like morning dew—the infamous co-signer. It was the perfect concoction. Just add another woefully unqualified applicant to the mix, stir and…Voilà! We have an approval, ladies and gentlemen.

"Well, I'm not signing off on this," I said, wrapped in moral indignation. "Besides, it'll be next door in three months. We both know it."

"Look, Kevin, there's only four days left in the month, and we still need to fund six million dollars to hit our goal. Just push it through."

"Just push it through…Jim, don't you find it strange that our only goal is to fund x amount of dollars each month? That there're no goals for keeping the default rate down? Doesn't anybody give a shit about that?"

"That's not our department. We approve and fund loans. The other side deals with payments and collections. Here, just give me the fucking file! Just get through the rest of the applications I left on your desk."

"Whatever," I said, handing him the file. I walked toward the door, pausing at the threshold, the gateway to the casino, then watched Jim pull a hundred-dollar pen from his shirt pocket and sign the loan. Approved!

You didn't have to be a genius to know the entire system was a house of cards. And that, one day, it would all come crashing down. Our metaphorical ship would spring a leak. The townsfolk would come for Dracula, with wooden stakes and dollar bills in their fat, greedy fingers.

I bought a sixpack of Lowenbrau after work, surreptitiously sucking them down as I drove in stop-and-go traffic down Interstate 15. Mari and I had rented an apartment in Normal Heights, the neighborhood of my youth. Living there provided a sense of comfort and familiarity. Yet as I sipped beer and snaked through traffic, it struck me as funny how I'd traveled so far and wide in my life, joining the Peace Corps and living overseas, only to be right back where I started from.

The only difference being, I had that corporate job now. The one I'd dreamed about in college while working toward a business degree, back when the pursuit of money and power seemed laudable. Admirable. But that was a lifetime ago, pre-Peace Corps, when my brain was wired differently. Yet here I was, years later, working my way up that same proverbial ladder. Hell, I'd even begun earning some decent money. I was on track. Moving toward a successful future. So, why did I feel a million miles from where I should be? I thought back to my time with Trout, of fighting evildoers and saving the world. But evil had returned. And it was near. The evil was my company. The evil was me.

The whooshing noise returned, flooding my ears. Deep, concussive shock waves that reminded me of my special waterfall in Nicaragua. The spot I'd slip off to whenever the world closed in. A place of respite and solitude. Where I'd tread water and allow an entire river to cascade down upon my head, clearing the sludge from my mind as I sank deeper and deeper into the lagoon. Whoosh, whoosh, whoosh!

I swallowed the last of beer number six while pulling up to our apartment. A wave of sadness flooded over me, like losing a best friend. Then panic set in, as I contemplated passing the rest of the night without booze, my mind twisting itself into a pretzel as it searched for a solution. How do I keep my promise to Mari of cutting back on my drinking while simultaneously filling the empty pit inside me?

Option F: *Fuck it!* won out. I drove to the liquor store, bought a pint of rum and headed to Hawley Point, a vacant strip of land overlooking Mission Valley and Interstate 8. Let's face it, I was weak, no better than my bank and its unquenchable thirst for blood and fresh victims. My thirst just happened to be for the sweet, sticky rum.

I parked my van sideways to get the best view, then jumped in the back and slid open the side door. There it was: the endless parade of red and white lights forever buzzing through a tangled web of freeways below. I pressed the rum bottle to my lips, excited by the feel of cold glass rubbing against my teeth and gums.

I peered down at the massive circuit board, electrical pulses traveling atop overloaded asphalt loops. A million ants scurrying home. Rushing from here to there, and from there to here. Rushing, rushing, rushing along. From nowhere to nowhere. Now I, too, was among their brethren. A fellow ant. An added pulse. A diode on the Motherboard.

Is this all that I am? All that *we* are? Isn't there something more? Or are we all just ants scurrying through life?

I took another swig of rum, allowing the liquid to burn as it flowed down my throat, warming the cavern inside my belly. Bob Marley sang, his melodic chants ringing into the night. And life became peaceful once more.

Hours later, I stumbled into the apartment and made a beeline for the bedroom. "Mari, Mari…wake up," I slurred. Her face scrunched up in anger. "Mari, I can't do this anymore…" I blurted, before she could unload on me for being a common drunk; An unremarkable, unoriginal, run-of-the-mill boozer. "I can't keep working a job I hate and living this fake life anymore."

"Como?" Mari's eyes were hollow and dark. Tired.

"I feel like I'm dying inside. Every day I sit in that fucking office. Every day I drive in that fucking traffic. Every day…Every fucking day. It's sucking the life out of me."

Mari shook her head in disgust. "What are you talking about? You wanted that job, and you've only been working there for six months. If you quit, what are we going to do for money? That's it, I'm getting a job. I don't care what you say."

"Come on, let's dance." I smiled and reached for her hand, my body swaying unsteadily. "Don't worry, I have a plan. You know I always have a plan."

"No, I will not dance with you! It's late and you're drunk again."

"I may be drunk, but I see the light."

I laid down next to her and closed my eyes. A minute later, the motherboard powered down.

Chapter 9

The lady behind the coffee counter pushed aside a streak of dark purple hair hiding her eyes, revealing a tiny silver stud poking up through her nostril. Which, strangely, I felt the urge to pick. "Can I help you?" she asked, peering up from some enormous, coffee-pouring contraption.

I made eye contact. "Just a medium coffee, please," then quickly turned away—not wanting to reveal my inner desire of excavating the silver from her nose. An archaeologist on a dig. Coffee had become 'cool' since I'd been away. Odd, how a drink I associated with my mom or grandma (drinking it over a game of pinochle or Scrabble), or with people like me, attempting to clear away the cobwebs after a heavy night of drinking—was all the rage now. They'd even invented a hundred new ways to drink it: Frappuccino, cappuccinos, Americano, cafe latte, macchiato, frappe, espressos. On and on. You were almost looked down upon if you ordered your basic humdrum cup of Joe.

"Here." She handed me an oversized mug of coffee, then disappeared behind a splash of purple hair.

I found a table in the corner and took a seat. My brain was throbbing, thumping from one side of cranial bone to the other. I'd really tied one on last night. I felt a pity party coming on. My job was a grind, confined for eight hours a day, buried up to my neck in sand, fire ants snapping at my face. I was tired and hadn't had a decent night's sleep in a decade. I couldn't take much more.

I stared into my coffee, studying the dark-brown liquid, so complex and full of character. A million stories lived within those chocolate swirls and amber rings. Powerful and robust stories. I dove into the rich mud and searched for the dark-red cherry at its heart. Solid and wise. Majestic.

***

I brush my fingers against the coffee beans. Skin upon skin. They're smooth and firm, and the hills are full of them. Cherry-red beans hidden inside the lush green foliage of the Caturra bush. Shaded by thick Sapote and Guanacaste branches. Banana leaves and palm fronds caressing their underbellies. Coffee in its natural state. Growing here in the jungles of Central America.

I'm once again amidst her beauty, a Peace Corps volunteer surrounded by a sea of green. Nature beating through my heart like a drum.

"Look!" Mitch called out. He was further ahead and pointing to a break in the jungle. We'd been working through vines and bushes for hours, and God only knows where Jason had disappeared to. Through the clearing, we saw three men feeding the red beans into a grinder. The motor wound up and down like an old-fashion siren each time they dumped in another bucketful. The grinder stripped away the outer husk, leaving a gooey seed which the men tossed into a large cement vat. The vat, filled with murky water, stretched out a good twenty feet. An old man, shirtless and sucking on a piece of straw, stirred the beans with a branch. His wiry arms, compact and muscular, never stopped mixing the dark soup.

Rotting husks and pulp covered the ground, at least two feet deep near the vat and the grinder. The men, buried up to their knees in the sludge. The smell was fierce, a mixture of rotting fruit and wet earth. Not horrible, but powerful. Pungent. Piercing straight through your nostrils.

Several boys were spread out among the rows of coffee, their little fingers—engines of dexterity—plucking beans from vines. When they filled their buckets, they raced to the grinder and dumped out their beans, then scurried back into the jungle.

My fingers slid against the red cherries, their smooth texture pulling me in. I wanted to press my cheeks against the soft berries and fade away.

"Dude, wake up! What are you sleepwalking?" Jason reappeared by my side.

"No, I, uh…Oh fuck off! Where in the hell have you been, anyway?"

"Looking for beer. Duh!"

"You realize we're in the middle of the fucking jungle, right?"

"No shit, Sherlock," Jason said, brushing banana leaves from his face. "Middle of fucking nowhere is more like it."

I'd been in the middle of fucking nowhere since joining the Peace Corps a year prior. After college, I found myself in a rut. The economy was in a recession, and my hard-earned sheepskin—my diploma—was little more than a keepsake. As I searched for a path forward, the Peace Corps, and its siren call to adventure, kept luring me in. One day, I succumbed. Veering off.

I was still trying to find my bearings over a year later in Nicaragua. Such a unique land, like walking into an adventure novel. Her beauty was raw and unrivaled. Learning Spanish and the different customs, the culture, had come with a series of failures. But the freedom Nicaragua offered…Ahh yes, the freedom…was unparalleled. I was living within nature, like I'd always wanted. Traveling from city to city, and country to country. Just as the Aztecs and the Mayans had done a thousand years before me. And it was amazing!

There'd been plenty of setbacks along the way, mostly during my three months of training, where I lived with an indigenous family in the small barrio of Monimbó. I'd tussled with my abusive host father; contracted Dengue Fever and nearly died; and was almost kicked out of the Peace Corps—on *several* occasions. More recently, after moving to Estelí—my permanent site in the northern Segovia Mountains—I'd been butting heads with my work counterpart, Bismarc, who turned out to be a real asshole. All this turmoil occurring while I adjusted to life in an unfamiliar country, alone and far away from the other volunteers in my group.

I'd met Mitch and Jason during our group's two-day orientation in Miami. The last two days in the States for quite some time. We found some commonalities: we were all from California, and we all liked to drink. Now here we were, a year later, traipsing through some remote coffee jungle in search of an ever-elusive border crossing. Rolling into our third week of a supposed two-week trek to the ancient Mayan ruins of Tikal. Our group of thirteen had been whittled down to ten, three volunteers packing up their shit and bailing. *¡No más!*

But not us. No, we were soldiering on. These excursions, like therapy, kept our spirits up. And soon, we'd be in Tikal, walking in the footsteps of Mayans. If we could ever find Guatemala!

El Salvador had been a sketchy piece of real estate to navigate. Lush and picturesque, but with a menacing undercurrent flowing through its air. El Salvador, like many countries in Central America, had seen plenty of bloodshed and civil war. Not hundreds of years ago, or even decades ago, but *years* ago. Fear waved upon every flagpole, the smell radiating out to every corner of the country.

El Salvador continued its march toward normalcy, the war etched into the faces of its people. Few smiled, and when they made eye contact, it was with a 'what-in-the-fuck-are-you-doing-here' stare. Shortly after nightfall, the people hunkered down, slamming shut metal gates and steel doors. The clanking of metal and clicking of locks sent shivers down our spines as we passed by, wondering if we were on the wrong side of the prison yard. We were ready to get out of El Salvador, if we could just find the fucking border.

"*¿Oye, chavalo, dónde está la frontera?*-Hey kid, where's the border?" Mitch hollered to a boy raking out coffee beans over a large slab of cement. Here's where the beans, golden yellow after being stripped of their dark-red outer husk and slimy inner skin, would bake in the sun for a week. And once completely dried, shoveled into burlap sacks stenciled *Café Arábica*, and exported around the world.

The boy giggled, then pointed to a grove of coffee bushes. "*Por allá, gringo*-Over there, whitey." The grinder's motor revved as we passed by. The men looked up as we stomped through the sludge, then went right back to work. I looked at the old man as we passed the soupy vat of beans, but he paid us little heed, just kept right on stirring. The aroma hung over the place like a cloud, drenching us in warm, earthy rot. We slipped into the grove where the boy had pointed and found a narrow path leading downhill. The coffee had grown so high, it was arching over and forming a tunnel. We pushed the branches aside, careful so they wouldn't snap back and hit the person behind us. A kilometer later, the jungle fell away. We spotted a yellow bar pointing toward the sky. Next to it, a guard shack with a rusty sign that said, "*¡Bienvenidos a Guatemala!*-Welcome to Guatemala!"

I turned and looked back toward the mountain, my eyes following the sway of the coffee and banana trees as they danced in the breeze. The caturra bushes sat resolute in the sun, its fat, red cherries clinging to its branches. Resilient. Powerful. Majestic.

"We should head straight to Tikal," Jason said. "We're way behind schedule."

"Schedule? Who the fuck's on a schedule?" I was having none of that. "No, we're going to the beach first, like we planned."

We turned to Mitch, our eastern philosophy guru. Buddha man. Having spent a year in China, we deemed him sufficiently qualified to make such important rulings, equating his quiet demeanor to a sense of inner wisdom. Mitch, ever the wise sage, looked from Jason to me, then up to the sky. And after a moment of reflection, he smiled and pulled out his trusty silver flask. "To the beach," he declared, taking a swig and passing it around. Problem solved. Buddha boy had spoken.

We got our passports stamped, adjusted our packs, and continued down the muddy path. Arriving in a village of thatch-roofed houses, where men huddled on porches carving animal and spirit figurines from slabs of mahogany and cherry wood. They wore thick jackets, woven of vibrant purple and indigo-blue thread. The tapping of their mallets and chisels reverberated off the walls, sending an echo throughout the town.

The men gave us a friendly nod, then returned to their clatter as we walked toward a fluorescent-green bus on the edge of town. They didn't speak Spanish, but a local dialect. A beautiful language of soft whispers and short sound bursts. These were descendants of the great Mayan civilization which once thrived in the nearby jungles, building intricate cities that sparkled like diamonds in a sea of green. A civilization which embraced their spiritualism and humanity, seeking answers to the deepest and most eternal questions posed to man: Why are we here? Why am *I* here?

We spent the rest of the day bouncing over rough roads as our colorful bus motored toward the coastal town of Monterrico. When the brakes finally squealed and the bus ground to a halt, I was sweaty and tired and eager to dive into the ocean.

"Where the hell's the beach?" I asked, so ready for a hammock and cold beer I could barely stand. But all I saw from my window was a thick marsh and jumble of boats bobbing in the dark water.

"We still need to cross the Chiquimulilla Canal," said Mitch, flipping through his Lonely Planet guidebook as we exited the bus.

Jason kicked at the dirt. "The Chiqui-wicki what?"

I sighed and lowered my head. We'd been traveling for weeks, and still had a long way to go to reach Tikal, our ultimate destination. My clothes were all dirty, smelling of stale sweat and ass. And I was skinny as a rail, subsisting on beer and rice. I needed the ocean like I needed air, to breathe life back into my lungs. To breathe life back into my soul.

"Come on, this will be fun," said Buddha boy.

Mitch was right, the boat ride was beautiful. The marsh was teeming with wildlife—turtles, iguanas, crabs. Pelicans soaring overhead as we cut through the swamp. Osprey and cormorants standing in the shallow water, spreading their wings and dipping their beaks in the water, fishing for a meal. Our boat wedged itself into the muddy banks of Monterrico. We strapped on our packs and sprinted toward the beach. I ripped off my pack and my shirt and dove into the ocean. The water was warm yet refreshing. Heavenly.

We swam for hours, washing away the dirt and grime and stench of travel. When our arms grew tired, we climbed into hammocks and napped, the ocean breeze cooling us. Breathing life back into our core.

In the evening, with the moon as our guide, we shuffled down the beach in our bare feet to the *Hideaway Cantina* to drink rum with our fellow travelers. The bar, a microcosm of the world, where people of all colors and creeds, all nationalities, and speaking every language, congregated for an evening of revelry. A boozy United Nations reeking of suntan lotion and pineapple.

And in keeping with the UN theme—of bridging cultural divides—I sought my own 'peaceful' connections, finding a friendly representative from France. A pretty Parisian with hair to her derriere. Our 'summit' lasted most of the night. The sun peeking up as I stumbled back to our hospedaje. I slept until noon, when the heat became too much to bear, then raced back into the ocean.

Day three arrived in a blink of an eye. It was time to move on. To complete the last leg of our journey to Tikal. As I stuffed dirty shirts and stinky socks into my pack, a calmness came over me. I heard the waves crashing in the distance, then the wind whistled, crisp and clear. I was present. In the moment. Zen wrapping me up in its cocoon.

"I'm staying," I blurted out, more to myself than anyone else.

"You're what?" Jason and Mitch's voices echoed.

"I'm staying. You guys go on without me."

"Dude, are you crazy?" Jason stood and cinched down the straps on his pack. "You're going to stay in Guatemala? By yourself?"

"Yep."

Mitch said nothing, just looked on, assessing the situation.

"What about going back?" Jason's cheeks turned red, and his lips formed a circle, the way they always did when he was trying to prove a point. "You're going to bus it all the way back through sketchy-ass El Salvador by yourself?"

"Yep."

"They're going to slice you up, man."

"Nobody's going to do shit to me." My mind was made up. Life was calling, and I was picking up.

Mitch fastened the last of his backpack straps to his waist and chest, and then we all stood silent for a moment. We'd each seen plenty of struggles since leaving the U.S. over a year ago, and these shared adventures sanded down the rough edges of being a Peace Corps volunteer. But it was time to part ways. Their adventure lay ahead in the magnificent Mayan ruins of Tikal. While I would stay here in Monterrico, soaking up the sun and the sea.

"A toast!" Mitch said, breaking the awkward silence. The steely flask made its appearance. And soon after, they walked off down the beach.

***

"More coffee?" The girl with the purple hair was standing above me.

I looked at my mug. The chocolate and amber swirls had disappeared, along with Jason, Mitch, and Guatemala. It had been a long time since I felt that freedom, a long time since I felt that alive. Part of something bigger than me. It was time to make a change. To find that young, adventurous man who stood alone on the shores of Monterrico. Pursuing something deeper inside. Something more profound. Answers to those Mayan questions…

Chapter 10

I rolled into work a new man. A man with purpose. Not even my massive hangover could bring me down. "Morning, Jim," I said with a big smile. He nearly fell over. Old, glum Kev was gone. I began approving every loan that Jim requested—no questions asked.

Our numbers soared over the next few months. Corporate loved us. Catering extravagant lunches with each target we met. As expected, the collection department grew and grew. Eventually, moving to its own floor to accommodate the new hires—temp workers, mainly, hired by outside companies in order to avoid giving out full benefits, even though most worked forty-hour weeks.

I came to realize I'd never be an outside sales agent. I'd proven myself too worthy a numbers assassin—slicing and dicing interest rates and basis points and pushing money out the door in record speed—to be let out of the office.

But I didn't give a shit. Not anymore. Nope, I didn't give a shit about Jim, or default rates, or corporate fucking ladders. Because I really did have a plan. Granted, it wasn't the most sophisticated of plans. But it was a plan, nonetheless. My *plan* was to save every single nickel and dime for one solid year, pack up my shit, and get the fuck out of Dodge, drive straight back to Nicaragua. Mari and I could open a restaurant, or a store, or some other business, and live out the rest of our lives in peace. Fuck the rat race! Fuck the ants! Fuck the electrical pulses, and circuit boards, and all the other drunken metaphors I'd invented to describe my unhappy existence. That was the plan. Simple. I just needed to execute it. Bring Mari onboard and proceed forward. How hard could that be?

Mari shit on my parade. Just more ramblings from a madman. "Every time you get drunk, you want to leave the country! Why don't you just stop drinking and maybe then you'll be able to appreciate it here? Besides, what are we going to do in Nicaragua? There's no money there. No jobs. Stop feeling sorry for yourself."

Mari had a way of drilling down to the core. No bullshit with her. She continued with her ESL classes during the evenings and submitted job applications to fast-food joints and retail stores during the day. She tolerated me over the next few weeks, barely, never really believing I was serious about moving back to Nicaragua.

My Monday-through-Friday grind continued. I was in a pit, with a prison cell being constructed around me. Day by day, and brick by fucking brick. My only solace, a glimmer of hope that this would all be in my rearview mirror someday; a distant memory fading into the dust as I crossed the Mexican border en route to a new life in Nicaragua, the dream alive once more.

I made the mistake of laughing one night when Mari mispronounced the word 'focus.' "Fuck us, fuck us," she kept saying. "Stop laughing!" she screamed, her face crimson. But it was no use. I had the giggles. She glared at me. "I'm never speaking to you in English again. Oh, and by the way, I'm not going to Nicaragua with you either. I'm staying right here."

My giggles came to an abrupt halt. Leaving the U.S. was the only thing holding me together. It was the duct tape preventing my innards from gushing out. The sutures holding my brain inside by skull. "What are you talking about? Mari…you have to go back. *We* have to go back. Can't you see that?"

"No, I don't see that. All I see is you drinking all the time. Why should I go anywhere with you?"

"Because if I stay here, I'm going to die…and because I love you."

Mari paced up and down the kitchen floor. Pissed! She was just getting started in America. Where she was thriving, I'd become a complete mess. Folding into myself at an alarming pace. She didn't deserve any of this. I was selfish for even asking her to go back. Why should she have to suffer just because I was too weak? Because I couldn't hack it?

"Mari, what if…"

"Stop talking! The only way I'll go back is if you stop drinking."

My mind scrambled. "Mari, I can't just stop drinking cold turkey like that. But I'll cut back. I'll cut *way* back, I promise. Just tell me you'll go with me."

She studied my eyes, searching for a twitch, a flutter, a darting pupil—all tells of the alcoholic. Easily found if you look close enough. Mari walked away. There was nothing more for her to say. The burden rested with me. I needed to step up and do my part. Stop being such a whiny little bitch.

And I did, mostly, over the next couple of months. I put the rum bottle down and stuck to beer. Became an obedient little rat, working my way through the maze each day and providing cheese to the masses. Cheese in the form of cash, which I knew would never be repaid. I sat dutifully in traffic every morning and every evening, remaining sober through it all. I even wrapped an entire roll of imaginary duct tape around my mouth to prevent the expletives, which swam around my head all day like sharks circling a seal, from bursting forth.

But when Friday rolled around, it was game on. I'd done my due diligence for the week, paid my penance, and was ready to get sideways. Ready to leave the rat race behind and get fucked up. But even then, I upheld my promise and steered clear of the sweet, tasty rum I loved so much. Sticking with beer. Although for some odd reason, the usual sixpack didn't quite cut it anymore. And I was drawn, more and more, to the twelve-pack section.

By month three, I realized I was in a slog. Shifting goals didn't necessarily equate to switching habits. Our finances were no better off than the day I concocted my exit-the-U.S.-at-all-cost strategy. My 'escape fund' was barely on life support. Even worse, I'd begun sneaking sips of rum whenever I found a dark corner and opportune moment, figuring I deserved this one small pleasure in life. This trivial gratification that made life bearable. Predictably, the sips turned to swallows, and the swallows to gulps. And before long, the whole 'cutting back' thing completely faded away. A distant memory.

VP Jim moved to a corner office, and I moved to a cubicle with a window. Joe Schmo got his doublewide and big plot of land in Pahrump, Nevada. Upward mobility at its finest. The American Dream primed and firing on all cylinders.

I returned to my customary sixpack of beer for the ride home, a sixpack being the perfect quantity for the hour-long drive. After exiting the freeway onto Adams Avenue, I made a pit stop in an alley to take a piss, then hit the liquor store for a bottle of dark rum. I'd graduated from a pint to a quart. I was a fucking pirate, after all.

From there it was off to Hawley Point to stare down at my fellow rats and drink until my eyes drooped. Until the miniature weights above my eyelids became too much to bear. I drank until my mind could no longer feel despair.

Until the neurons ferrying desperation and cynicism ceased to leap across the synapses of my brain. I drank until a dull, empty void permeated my being. Until I felt nothing.

Stumbling through the door, I caught sight of Mari standing in the living room with her hands on her hips. The dark shade of red on her face, such a stark contrast to her usual dark-chocolate Mayan skin. *"Dónde estaba!"* she spat, her eyes beads of black coal.

I swayed, putting my hand against the wall to steady myself. "What…it's only 10 o'clock. What's the big fucking deal?"

"You said you were going to stop drinking!" The coal ignited, fire pouring from her eyes.

"Correction," I slurred. "I said I'd *cut back* on my drinking."

"Oh, so this is what you call cutting back? *¡Eres un puto borracho!*"

"Correction, I'm not a bitch and a drunk. I'm just a drunk. *You*, my dear, are a bitch." I slid down on the couch, trying to disappear, waiting for the smack to my head or across my face. Mari hovered above me, contemplating her next move. But I was seeing two of her by then; and having a hard time figuring out which one to look at.

"I'm not going to Nicaragua with you. I'm not going anywhere with you. Ever."

"Oh, what's the big deal? I work in a freaking cubicle all day and just want a little drink after work. Is that so bad? Give me a fucking break."

"Kevin…" Her tone softened, the beads of fire now filled with sadness and despair.

"Look, I'm sorry. I just need a break from all the bullshit sometimes. It's so hard sitting in that fucking building all week like some caged animal. When I get off work, it feels like I'm escaping, like I'm finally free. It feels like I'm in Nicaragua again."

"But you promised."

"I *have* cut back. I mean…a little."

"No, you haven't. You just drink more on the weekends. And now you're drinking during the week again. You drink more than you did before you made your stupid promise!"

I wanted to hug her, to tell her that everything was going to be all right. Let her know I'd get my drinking under control. And that in nine months, or a year, or whenever, we'd escape this death sentence hanging over me. I wanted to tell her there was still hope, and that I loved her, and really did have a plan. But in reality, I wanted a drink so bad I could feel it worming its way through my brain. A ravenous dog in search of blood.

My fingers clenched tight around the rum bottle. Target acquired. The crinkling of the brown paper bag comforted me, like a mom tucking in her child. Everything slowed. Mari continued to talk. But I no longer heard her words. A war had broken out inside my cerebral cortex. Neurons clashing with neurons. Opposing forces. One commanding me to drink, the other attempting to paralyze my arm. I focused in on Mari, ignoring the incoming salvo from the enemy. Just wait, I told myself. Let her finish saying everything she's been waiting to say and goes to bed before you drink.

But I didn't wait. Didn't even turn around and face away. Just lifted the bottle and chugged away. Letting the sweet rum splash down my throat as Mari looked on in disgust. The glug-glugging drowned out her voice completely. The warm sensation in my stomach, like life itself. Like being back in the womb. Whoosh, whoosh!

Mari's voice rose above the din. "Go drink your fucking *guaro*. I don't care anymore." She stormed out of the apartment, slamming the door in her wake. I tried to follow but stumbled and fell to the floor. She probably just needed time to cool down. What a fucking mess. Finishing the last of the rum, I staggered into the kitchen, hoping to find a beer or some other form of alcohol. *Can't a guy just have a drink?* On the table was a thick steak and a mound of rice, cold and sad looking. I'm such an asshole!

Chapter 11

My friendship with Trout continued to grow. We became inseparable, hanging out nearly every day. But love remained on my trail, a bloodhound on a scent.

The bell rang, kids dashing to the blacktop for one last game of tag before the weekend. Trout and I played a few games of tetherball before sprinting away from John Adams Elementary. We raced past Fire Station 18, and across the manicured lawns of St. Didacus Parish, where the Catholic kids went to school. Rounding the corner to Trout's apartment, I spotted Carla standing in front of a stucco wall. My head whipped around, followed by my body, causing me to stumble down the alley like I'd just been clotheslined by an NFL linebacker.

Miraculously, I regained my balance. Hunched over and panting, I looked up and into the eyes of heaven. The earth shifted on its axis, spinning faster than it ever had.

Carla giggled, revealing two side teeth that stuck out further than the rest, creating the cutest smile I'd ever seen. My face burned red hot. And I was positive the entire neighborhood could hear my heart thumping away inside my chest. I looked down, pretending I hadn't seen her—pretending like it wasn't me who'd just been stumbling down the alley. Wishing I was a magician so I could make myself disappear.

"Just learn to walk?" The voice hadn't come from Carla, but from her best friend, Regina, whom I hadn't noticed standing, or rather, lurking, in the shadows. She scanned me up and down with disgust. "What are *you* doing here?" Regina started, her voice brimming with disdain. "You don't belong…" But then her gaze shifted off me. "Oh…hey, Trout," she called out, her tone markedly softer. I sighed, knowing I was no longer her prime target.

"Hey," Trout replied, his voice trailing off like he'd just been called to the principal's office.

Regina's eyes returned to me, lasers traveling up and down my body. Sizing up my ratty shoes and goofy clothes. Mom, unable to afford the Nike shoes and surf clothes that were all the rage, had handpicked my wardrobe from K-mart.

Regina made a dismissive grunt and turned away. I was a zero in her book. Not even worth the bother. I turned back to Carla, knee bent, foot resting against the textured wall. She was so beautiful. I scanned my brain, searching for something to say. A witty sentence, a word…a sound. But nothing came. Only a swarm of butterflies taking flight inside my belly.

"Come on," Trout said, tapping me on my shoulder, "let's go watch the end of Speed Racer."

I followed him into the apartment complex, Carla disappearing from view. As he started up the stairs, I called out, "Hey, you wanna play outside today?"

"Later," he said from the top of the stairs. "We'll miss *The Twilight Zone*."

I bounded up the stairs two steps at a time, catching him at the front door. "Come on, man, let's just play outside. We could ride your bike up and down the alley."

He pulled a long string from around his neck and gripped the key on it. "Oh man, don't tell me you like Regina."

"No fucking way!"

"Yeah, you do."

"No, I don't!"

Trout paused for a moment, then smirked. "Ooh…so it's Carla."

"No," I mumbled, unconvincingly.

"Ha! So, it is Carla." He unlocked the door, and I followed him inside.

"Let's just play outside. What's the big deal? We can watch TV anytime."

"Love, exciting and new, come aboard…" Trout began singing the theme to *The Love Boat* while turning on the TV.

"Ahh, shut the fuck up!" I shot back.

He turned and saw me pouting by the front door. His face softened. "Alright, alright, let's go. But I'm not hanging out with Regina!"

We grabbed his bike and wheeled it into the alley. My smile all but collapsed when I didn't see Carla and Regina. I jumped on the bike and flew up the alley, cranking hard on the pedals. Tires spinning, wind whipping through my hair, buildings zipping by. Reaching the end of the alley, I yanked the handlebars to the side and slammed on the brakes. The back tire slid out, leaving a long, arcing skid mark. Trout was but a mere dot in the distance. A speck of dust in the infiniteness of space. I wanted to keep pedaling. To keep moving. To travel around the world, and through the universe, absorbing light and energy. Forever in motion.

I spun the bike around and rode, pedaling harder and harder. A rocket ship hurtling through space. Trout grew with each pump of my legs. Laughter bounced off the walls as I approached. Following the sound, I spotted Carla and Regina peering down at me from an upstairs window. I pretended not to see them, attempting to pop a wheelie. Trout came near, holding out his hand for the bike. But I zipped around him and sped off. "Hey," he shouted, as I raced back up the alley, "it's my turn!"

I only rode halfway up the alley before turning back and popping another feeble wheelie as I approached the girls' window. Trout blocked my path, and I reluctantly handed over the bike. He pedaled off, leaving me alone, under the searing gaze of Carla and Regina. I stared at the back of Trout's shirt as he rode away, my head frozen, my inner voice repeating, "Don't look up! Don't look up! Don't look up!" My eyes disobeyed my brain's command, slowly climbing the stucco wall in search of Carla.

"Hey, what's your name?" Regina called down. I quickly averted my eyes, affixing a death stare on Trout. "Hey," she repeated, much louder this time. "I said, what's your name!"

The ice block on my neck, keeping my head pointed forward, cracked and fell away. I finally turned and hollered "Kevin," much louder than I meant to. I could see them in the window just as clear as day. Carla was smiling, her two pointy teeth on full display.

"You guys want to come up and hang out?" Regina asked.

My heart sped up, racing at Mach-5. "Uh…uh…let me ask Trout."

"Uh…uh…ok," Regina parroted back. Carla still hadn't spoken. I knew her voice would be sweet. That *she* would be sweet. I could tell just by looking at her. By her smile and her laugh. She just had to be. There was no way she would be mean like Regina.

When Trout came zipping back, I nearly knocked him off his bike in my excitement. "Hey, man," I said breathlessly, "they want us to come up."

"Who?"

I pointed to the window. "Them!"

Trout's trademark smirk returned, spreading across his milky-white skin. He made a loose fist with his fingers and play punched my arm. "Well, look at you."

"Shhhh," I whispered, pushing his hand away.

My knees felt like mush as we climbed the stairs. Regina opened the door and led us into the living room, the lair of the tigress, where she once again looked me over. Staring at me as if I were some bum off the street. "So," she finally said, "where did *you* come from?"

I thought about the question, and the myriad of answers that grew from it. Endless possibilities like the branches of a tree. I could have said Pascagoula, Mississippi, where I lived for a stint that time Mom uprooted us from our lives to go 'wherever the road takes us.' Or Long Beach, where I lived with my uncle Mike and aunt Carol for a spell while Mom knocked back vodkas on one of her extended drinking binges.

I could have said I came from Pomona, where I lived with my aunt Sheila while Mom was being 'treated.' Or even University Heights, where I'd lived with my grandma at different times over the years. In fact, I could have told Regina any number of places I'd 'come from' over the first twelve years of my life, bouncing like a ball from home to home. But I went with the most recent, the place I'd found a measure of solace while roaming through its mountains. "Santee," I said firmly.

"Well, don't they have shoes in Santee?" Regina snickered.

I looked down at my shoes, my face beet red, wishing I was no longer there. I tried tucking them underneath me, performing a pirouette. I stole a glance at Carla, noting how she wasn't smiling, reaffirming my belief that she was nice. She wasn't the type of person who cared if I wore Nikes or Vans. She'd understand that the reason my shoes wore out so fast was because I was always skateboarding and bike riding and adventuring through canyons.

"Leave him alone," Trout barked, "he's cool." I felt a weight come off. Trout had my back. My eyes traveled back to Carla. She wore a lavender OP blouse with red hibiscus flowers on one shoulder, and a white, long-sleeved thermal underneath. Her blonde hair, feathered on the sides, fell lazily just past her shoulders. A handful of freckles danced across her tan cheeks and nose whenever she smiled.

I looked around. A white sofa wrapped around the living room. Behind it sat a silver tray with an array of crystal bottles. Regina followed my eyes. Then, with a grin, "You want a drink, Santee boy?"

"What is it?"

"It's booze, dummy. Haven't you ever seen a bar before?"

"Yes," I said, even though I hadn't. At least not any bar like that. Now, Trout and I had spent plenty of time inside an actual bar, Tuba Man's, and seen plenty of liquor bottles. But never in fancy crystal containers spread out on a silver tray.

"So, do you want a drink or not? Maybe you're just chicken." And there it was, that fucking word. Add it to all the others: pussy, scaredy-cat, bitch. Each equating to the same thing. And whenever I heard one, it made my blood boil.

"Fuck no, I'm not chicken. Pour me one!"

Regina walked behind the sofa, grabbed a glass off the tray and filled it a quarter of the way with an auburn liquor from one bottle. Walking toward me, she held out the glass. "So, drink up then."

I snatched the glass from her hand, then stared into the liquid. It reminded me of root beer without the fizz. I put my nose to the rim and breathed in. It smelled like gasoline, only stronger. I'd always liked the smell of gasoline, and how it made me feel dizzy whenever Mom filled up the tank. But I never would've drunk it!

I looked at Trout, his eyes wide with concern. Then to Carla, whose eyes expressed compassion. "You don't have to drink that," she said. Her words melted my heart, so soft and sweet, just as I'd predicted.

"Yes, he does," commanded Regina.

"Just leave him alone," Carla shot back.

I swirled the alcohol around in the glass. Whoosh, whoosh. Then gulped down the entire drink. It burned, liquid fire oozing through my gullet. I let out a sigh, a dragon breathing fire. Beads of sweat formed on my brow, and my hands were clammy.

Regina poured another glass, a reddish elixir this time, and all the way to the brim. The funny thing was, I no longer feared her. Or even despised her. She was a zero in *my* book now. Not even worth the bother. She took a sip and passed it to Carla, whose lips turned a dark shade of red when she drank. Next up was Trout. By the time the glass made its way back to me, I was euphoric and eager for more.

My body felt warm and safe with each drink, like sitting in front of a fire on a chilly night. I no longer gave a rat's ass about my beat-up, no-name tennis shoes. Or my cheap K-mart clothes and messy hair. I could have cared less where I *came* from, or all the shit I'd been through over the past few years. No, all I cared about was right here and right now. And Carla, the most beautiful girl in the world.

We began chasing each other around the apartment. Racing in and out of rooms, through the kitchen, circling the couch. Laughing at the top of our lungs. Four drunken fifth graders without a care in the world. We eventually fell to the ground, exhausted. Seconds later, the room began to spin. Round and round like a horse on a carousel. We grabbed fistfuls of carpet and held on tight as the ceiling became a pinwheel. Reaching for a thicker chunk of carpet, my fingers brushed against Carla's. The connection was electrifying. She slid her hand in mine, and for a moment, all was right with the world.

Trout and I remained best friends, inseparable, over the next two years. But when middle school arrived, he moved on to charter school, while I entered one of the roughest schools in San Diego. And in time, our friendship faded, as all things do.

I sometimes wonder about the night we almost burned down the laundromat, and the mess the owner found the next day as he pulled gobs of wet, singed mail from his mail slot. Did he realize how close he'd come to losing his entire business? Of having everything burned to the ground by two idiot, ten-year-old delinquents? Probably not.

Tuba Man's, ironically, burned to the ground ten years later. The flames reducing a lifetime of memorabilia to a pile of ash and soot in less than an hour. The golden tuba would exist no more. The fire chief said the cause of fire was arson. Fortunately, I had a solid alibi, muddling through college some six hundred miles to the north. Now, the whereabouts of Trout at the time… Unknown!

Carla and I barely spoke after our drunken day together. Each of us painfully shy in matters of the heart. The following year, she moved away. And while I pined for Carla and wished upon all the stars that she would have become my girlfriend. It was of little consequence. As life had revealed that Carla was *not* my first love.

No, sadly, that distinction belonged to alcohol, booze…the witch's brew. And oh, what a powerful love she'd prove to be, holding sway over me for years to come. Cupid's arrow had found his mark, reaching to the very bone.

Chapter 12

Things had changed between Mari and me since our blowup. She no longer looked at me with the same loving eyes, but with disdain and anger. Pity. Perhaps even a touch of sorrow for what used to be. My stupidity hung heavy around my neck, a yoke of shame, which I alone held the key. Yet I couldn't steady my hand long enough to release my burden. To reap the riches of the world.

Mari sat at the kitchen table, engrossed in her English books. She didn't even look up when I came in. It had been a long day at work. One of those days that feels more like an eternity.

"Hola," I said, digging through the cupboards for some food. She continued writing vocabulary words in her notebook as if I were invisible: *mountain, river, forest, trees, fish, bear…*

"Hola," I repeated. Mari stared straight ahead, scribbling frantically: *tree, branches, cabin, moon, wolf…*She was pissed off. And tired. Tired of me complaining about my job. Tired of me drinking. Tired of my inability to adjust to life in the U.S.

And who could blame her? After coming from one of the poorest countries in the Western Hemisphere, not speaking the language, technology beyond anything she'd ever known, she'd adjusted to life in San Diego. Learning the bus system, making friends with other students from her ESL classes, and submitting job applications to restaurants and cleaning companies throughout San Diego. She was on fire while I was drowning in an ocean of self-pity. Mari loved San Diego. And what's not to love? Amazing weather, abundant financial opportunities, friendly neighborhoods, beaches…

What the *fuck* was my problem?

"Mari, I need to get away for a couple of days. To clear my head." I didn't bother giving her the details of my 'latest and greatest' plan. She'd heard enough of my shit before. I just hoped she'd still be there when I got back.

Mari didn't move, not even a flutter, immune to my inadequacies by then.

Early the next morning, as I stuffed a pair of trunks and a towel into my backpack, I felt a strength mounting inside me, like a soldier preparing for battle. I grabbed my surfboard and headed for the front door. Walking out, I turned and shouted, "I love you," toward the bedroom. My words rang hollow, echoing across a bottomless chasm. Lonely words, dissipating into the ether. Leaving only silence, deafening silence.

Ensenada is a megacity about an hour's drive south of San Diego in Mexico's Baja California Norte. The city has a bustling port and thriving business center. But is more widely known—at least among gringos—for its popular Hussong's Cantina, complete with screaming parrot and raucous party crowds. But for me, Ensenada represented an obstacle, a traffic nightmare, which I was forced to drive through in order to reach my beloved stretch of coastline five hours to the south.

To make matters worse, it was a fifty-fifty shot whether I'd be pulled over and shaken down each time I drove through the city. Because, for some illogical reason, the Ensenada engineers had routed the highway directly through the city. Forcing all cars to drive through the center of the third largest city in Baja California if they wanted to continue their journeys north or south.

Lady luck was on my side, and I maneuvered through Ensenada without incident. A few kilometers later, the Pacific Ocean came into view, the blue beauty stretching out to the horizon. Mari, my work, feeling confined—all fell away like glaciers sliding into the sea. Excited, I punched the gas. The VW sputtered, then cranked up to 60 mph. I was really flying, even hitting 70 on the downhills.

About an hour south of Ensenada, I pulled into a *Sub Agencia,* where you can purchase beer in bulk and at a steep discount. I bought two cases of *Pacífico* and three giant bags of ice, then walked across the dirt lot to the *Licoria,* where I bought two bottles of Tequila and a bottle of Kahlua. I was ready for my weekend of solitude, my plan officially in motion.

I stuffed as much beer and ice as would fit into the old cooler I kept next to the driver's seat, then hopped back on Highway 1 South. An hour later, I spotted a man walking along the freeway with two guitars strapped to his back and his thumb out. "*Pase, pase,*" I said, pulling up alongside.

"*Gracias, gracias,*" he replied, climbing into the van with a smile.

He situated himself and his guitars as I pulled back onto the pavement. His eyes fell to the beer in my hand, and the smile quickly faded. "*¿Quieres una?*" I offered, grabbing a beer from the cooler and holding it up as a peace offering. He shifted in his seat uncomfortably and looked away. I was working on my sixth or seventh beer by then. I'd lost count. And my driving skills were beginning to reflect it. The road had narrowed considerably, and was so badly pockmarked and scarred, it appeared a WWII bomber had dropped its payload on it overnight. The crumbling asphalt forced me to bob and weave like a boxer, swerving back and forth and in and out, as I struggled to avoid the craters and blackholes eager to swallow us up.

"You sure?" I asked Mr. Guitar man, waving a *Pacífico* in my right hand, while maneuvering through land mines with my left.

"*No, gracias,*" he said firmly, shaking his head for added emphasis. My attempt to put him at ease had failed. "*Y a dónde vas*-So, where are you going?" I inquired.

He braced his hand against the dash. "Cabo San Lucas." After some further coaxing, I learned he was traveling to the tip of the Baja Peninsula to sell his guitars, both of which he'd made by hand. I glanced back at the guitars, admiring their craftsmanship. He'd fashioned them from a light, blonde wood that highlighted the patterns in the grain. The neck and bridge were darker, perhaps cherry or teakwood, making for a beautiful contrast.

"Play some guitar," I commanded, reaching for one of the two instruments.

"*¡Cuidado!*" the man shouted, pointing to a pothole the size of Vermont. I zipped around it and motored on, my heart barely registering the close call.

"*¿Y cuánto tiempo para llegar a Cabo?*-And how long does it take to get to Cabo?"

Before he could answer, a giant gash in the pavement was upon us. I swung the van hard to the right, driving onto the shoulder and kicking up a cloud of dirt.

Just outside our window, a cliff plunged a hundred feet into the sea. My passenger's eyes grew as big as silver dollars, looking from me to the rocky ocean below. I heaved the steering wheel to the left and scrambled back onto the pavement. My heart was racing then.

"*¿Ahora quieres una?*-Now you want one?" I asked, reaching for another beer, unfazed by our near-death experience.

"*¡Aquí, aquí! ¡No más! ¡Dejame aquí!*-Here, here! No more! Leave me here!" My hitchhiker's eyes were now as big as teacup saucers.

"Oh, come on, man, that was an accident. Don't be such a pussy."

"*Por favor, señor!*" the man pleaded.

"Okay, okay…fine…just relax." I pulled the van into an empty patch of dirt in literally the middle of nowhere. "You sure you want to get out here? I can drive you to the next town. Don't worry, I'll drive better. I promise."

He clutched his duffel bag to his chest and scrambled out of the van, moving so quickly he stumbled and fell to the ground. I felt like a serial killer releasing my prey.

"Hey…don't forget your guitars."

He stood, reached into the van, and snatched the guitars off the floorboard. Then he turned and half speed-walked, half sprinted down the highway, traveling in the opposite direction of Cabo San Lucas, miles from civilization.

I pulled up to a taco stand in the next town and ordered five carne asada tacos, piling them high with onion and cilantro, then drowning them in hot sauce. Maybe I was a little drunk. I scarfed down all five in just a few minutes. The food felt good inside my belly, helping me focus. I still had a long drive ahead and needed to pace myself. I fired up the van and drove on.

Five hours later, I pulled off the freeway and rumbled down a narrow dirt road for a mile or two. After cresting a bluff, the beautiful Pacific Ocean came into view. I'd reached my secret spot of El Socorro. The best part, not another living soul for miles. Peace and fucking quiet. Solitude!

I set up camp, collecting driftwood along the shore. Then, when everything was neat and orderly, I started a bonfire, feeding it until it was a massive blaze. Then I grabbed the first bottle of tequila, cranked up Yellowman, and got down to business. The first swallow was euphoric—electric—like the day I touched Carla's fingers.

I stared into the flames, attempting to center myself in the world. Just past the fire, the sun was fading below the horizon. A bloody orb melting into the sea. I drank more tequila, embracing the darkness. Columns of smoke billowed from the blaze, sentinels guarding my sanity. Erasing the chaos.

I'd sat in this exact same spot years prior, doing the exact same things: drinking Tequila like water, staring into the fire, searching for some 'force' to guide me in the right direction. Incredibly, it had worked, nudging me off my trajectory and setting me on a fresh path. A path that would lead me to join the Peace Corps, which changed the way I viewed the world.

I hugged the Tequila bottle to my chest hoping for that same inspiration to reappear. To guide me on a fresh path. But the sky was silent. The stars and moon, the planets, continued on. Indifferent to my Earthly plight.

I raised the Tequila bottle to the fire, staring at the clear liquid inside. Such a magical, hypnotic elixir. I swirled it around, mesmerized by the miniature waves that sloshed inside, forever under its spell.

A spell teleporting me back to that cool, autumn night when Mom slapped me across my face. I remembered how my cheek burned, the molten lava, but it paled compared to the fire that raged inside me. A hatred that no amount of water could quell. And as I stood there quietly hating my mother, my mind shifted back to that day with Carla years before. The day I first drank alcohol. I remembered how it made me feel. Like being cloaked in armor. Like being invincible!

So, later that night, after Mom had gone to bed, I tiptoed across the patio to an old wooden cabinet where my stepdad stored his booze. I opened the doors slowly, freezing at every squeak of a hinge, prying back the Ark of the Covenant. Inside, the lab of an alchemist, with bottles of every shape and size, containing liquids of every color: greens, oranges, reds, blues, browns, clear.

I reached for the plainest, most nondescript bottle, then slipped into the alley. Once clear of the house, I sprinted toward the nearby canyon. After hopping a metal barrier and scaling a chain-link fence, I maneuvered through chaparral and sagebrush, finding a hidden spot overlooking the 805 Freeway. Then I slid down on my ass, hidden from the world.

I took a long, full swallow. The burn felt good, just how I remembered it. A wildfire spread inside my stomach. Then my head swam. Moments later, I drifted away. Up into the stratosphere. Laughing at life and all the bullshit. All so meaningless. All so trivial.

Chapter 13

When I woke, I was in El Socorro. The fire still smoldered, clinging to its last breath of life. I put on my wetsuit, grabbed my surfboard, and hobbled down to the shore, my head still reeling from the night before. The ocean was glassy and calm, with a perfect line of swells rolling in. I paddled out into the freezing water and caught a quick, chest-high wave, slicing through the translucent ocean and kicking out the back. A beautiful purple and baby-blue sunrise peeked up from the east, while dozens of seagulls and herons dove into the ocean less than a hundred feet from where I sat on my board. It was a perfect day.

I squared around to catch another wave but became lightheaded and nauseous. Then I puked all over my board and down the front of my wetsuit. Chunks of undigested carne asada, cilantro, tequila, and bile floated around me in the ocean. I paddled away from the stinky mess and caught the next wave in, body boarding it back to shore.

When I reached the van, I grabbed the brown bottle of Kahlua and chugged it down. Breakfast of champions! Fuck surfing. I had other priorities.

Later that afternoon, an old, rusty El Camino rattled down the road and parked nearby. A local man got out, grabbing a bucket, an empty milk jug, and a net from the back of his car. He waded into the ocean, towing his items through the water with a rope he tied around his waist.

For the next hour, while I put away one Pacifico after the other, the man dove into the sea, often staying under for two minutes or longer. When he surfaced, he stayed above the water just long enough to catch his breath and stuff his net with items I couldn't make out.

I was feeling nice and tipsy by the time he made his way up the sand. "*¿Oye amigo, qué hacías allá?*-Hey, buddy, what were you doing out there?"

He held open his net, which was stuffed full of bright-red lobsters opening and closing their claws, confused to be out of the water for the first time.

"Oh, man, that's awesome. What are you going to do with all of them?"

"Sell them to local restaurants." He slung the net over his dark-brown shoulder and began walking away.

"Wait, can I buy some from you?" I asked excitedly.

"Claro," he said.

I bought three spiny lobsters, all over two feet long, for the grand sum of $10. After high fiving the diver, I boiled up some water and spent the rest of the day eating chunks of scrumptious lobster while polishing off the last of the Pacíficos.

Just before sunset, I threw the last stack of driftwood into the firepit and got another bonfire blazing. Then I sunk into my beach chair, my fingers clenched tight around the last bottle of tequila. The alcohol drained away, and soon my body was plunging, skidding through the canyon of my youth. When I came to a halt, I saw my thirteen-year-old-self, drinking no-name booze while watching the moon overhead. I wondered what he was thinking—what *I* was thinking—staring up at the moon. Did he have hope? I wish I could have talked to that boy. Let him know things would get better.

Then I was that boy, blurry and immune to pain, staggering up the canyon. It was early morning when I pushed down, ever so gently, on the patio-gate latch, careful not to wake Mom I tiptoed across the patio, not making a sound, and was almost in the clear—just a few feet from my door—when I kicked over a rake. It rattled across the cement and hit a wall. I froze, hoping against all hope that nobody would wake, that they were all in a deep slumber.

My heart pounded as I tried to slow my breathing, taking in deep breaths. A minute passed and nothing happened. No movement. I was in the clear! I took another step toward my door when Mom's light turned on. FUCK!

What to do? What to do?

Run!

I rushed toward my door, turning the handle and flinging it open. But just as I was crossing the threshold to safety, Mom appeared like a ghost from the underworld. "And just what in the hell are you doing?" Her voice was low and guttural, sending a chill up my spine.

I turned and faced her. "Nuh…nuh…nothing," I mumbled.

Her eyes narrowed, a panther sizing up its prey. "Are you just getting home from somewhere?"

"No!" I blurted out. "I was just, uh, get…get…getting some air." I tried hiding my drunkenness, but my body felt like a sequoia in a windstorm, swaying back and forth as hundred-mile-per-hour gusts shot through my canopy.

"Okay, so you're outside in the middle of the night just *get…get…getting some air*, huh?" She scanned me up and down, a human x-ray machine searching for the cancer. "You're full of shit. Where were you?"

"No…uh…I…I…was…"

"Come closer," she demanded.

I took a half step forward, holding my head to the side so she wouldn't catch a whiff of my boozy breath.

"Closer!"

I took another step forward, a baby step, while tilting my head and trying to maintain my balance.

Mom tilted her head as well, matching my own awkward angle, then growled, "Breathe on me."

"What?" I feigned confusion, my heart racing.

"You heard me, I said breathe on me."

I turned my head slightly and let out a poof of air. An infinitesimal spritz of molecules. Negligible, really. But that cluster of particles, that spatter, held a tornado within its core. A tornado of vodka or gin or whatever the fuck I'd been drinking down in that canyon.

Mom's face compressed, engorging the thick vein that ran across her forehead. "Why, you little shit!" she spat, her eyes dilated, toxic pools of green. "You've been drinking."

I shifted my weight, hoping to counteract gravity, which seemed intent on dropping me to the ground. "No, I…"

"How much did you drink?"

"None!" I screamed, as no-name-liquor vapors sailed through the air.

"Don't fucking lie to me, you smell like a god damn distillery! Where in the hell have you been?" Her eyes shot from me to the liquor cabinet and then to the gate, processing the scene like a seasoned detective. "Where's the bottle?"

"What bottle?" I asked, acting dumb but smiling inside, knowing the bottle would never be found, as I'd chucked it as far down the canyon as humanly possible.

"Wait, let me get this straight," Mom's index finger pushed into my chest, "my 13-year-old son is already drinking."

Alcohol was taking over my body. Invasion of the Body Snatchers. "Wh…wh…what?" I attempted to respond.

"And you're drunk! How special. My 13-year-old son is drunk in the middle of the night."

I raised my head and stared into her eyes, swaying from side to side, searching for equilibrium. The fire I'd felt in the canyon came roaring back, heating my core. I no longer gave a shit if she knew I was drunk. Alcohol was my shield, providing cover from all pain.

"Say something!" she demanded.

A smile crept across my face. "Well, I had a pretty good fucking teacher!"

I clenched my teeth and waited. Waited for the slap. Relishing the moment. I wanted to feel the sting, the burn, the sweet taste of blood as it coated my mouth. The throbbing in my gums as they scraped against my teeth. I took in a deep breath of air, then arched out my chin as far as it would go. Right fucking here!

***

A gust of wind came off the ocean, rousing me from my drunken stupor. The fire was still going strong, crackling and popping as I lounged in my chair. A rustling in the bushes made me sit up straight. My ears shifted into red alert, scanning the area with sonar precision. Bloop, bloop, bloop, bloop. I heard more rustling, closer this time. The hairs on my arm pricked up. I grabbed the Tequila bottle by its neck and squeezed.

A man emerged from the brush and stood by the fire. I squeezed the bottle tighter, ready to strike with my glass club. Fight or flight? Fight or flight? Fight or flight?

The man pushed his wavy blonde hair behind his ears and said, "What's up, chief?"

Fight! "Where the fuck did you come from?" I said, ready to spring forward. I may have been fucked up, but I was more than capable of swinging a tequila bottle at blondie's head.

"From just up the road, man. It's all good. What about you, brother? What are you doing here?" The fire cast an orange glow upon his face, lighting up his eyes, pale green with red rims.

"I'm camping," I waved my hand around my campsite, like showing off a bedroom set on *The Price is Right*. "Can't you see that?"

The man didn't look around, just stood there, tall and relaxed, as if he'd been there his entire life. His reddish-blonde beard, reflecting the light of the fire, appeared to be on fire. I looked past him to the bushes where he'd emerged. "Hey, how did you get here? I didn't hear a car."

He slid his fingers along the side of his beard as if strumming a guitar. "How does anybody get anywhere?"

"Wait, what?" I puffed out my chest, posturing. "Hold on, man. What are you doing here? Are you camping around here or something?"

"Hey, take it easy, chief. I just want to know what *you're* doing here?" He held out his hands, palms up, and tilted his head to the side.

"I just told you; I'm camping."

"Camping, huh? You sure about that?"

"Yeah, I'm sure. Camping, surfing…" I held the Tequila bottle up to the fire. "Drinking!" The booze splashed inside, miniature waves of joy, while less than a hundred feet lay the ocean and its endless parade of waves crashing against the shore. The constant barrage, Mother Nature's timeless battle, made everything else seem trivial. Meaningless.

The air was thick with smoke, and the smell of the sea was all around. I pointed a finger at the mystery man, his beard afire and eyes aglow. "What about you…what are *you* doing here?"

"Aw, man, I'm just traveling. Bouncing around. Zip-a-dee-doo-dah." He hopped from one foot to the other, kicking his toes together like some fucking leprechaun.

"Zip-a-dee-A," I said, finishing his song. And in that moment, I questioned my sanity. What *was* I doing there? Alone in Mexico on a deserted stretch of coast, without my wife, the woman I supposedly loved, whom I'd taken thousands of miles away from her family and friends. From her country. From her life. The woman I'd left in San Diego while I got silly drunk and babbled idiocies to some giant Norse leprechaun?

What the fuck was my plan again? How was this furthering my long-term objectives? Blondie stepped closer to the fire. "Wait a minute," I said. "Who the hell are you?"

"Oh, I'm Vek. Who are you?"

"So, where in the hell did you come from, Vik?"

He took another step toward the fire. "It's not Vik, it's Vek, and I came from just up the road. But I ask again, who are you?"

"And what's up the road?" I asked, spinning the cap off the Tequila bottle and sucking down drops of heaven.

He chuckled, then squatted down and poked the embers with a branch. "What's up ahead? Hmm?" He stroked his chin like a professor solving a problem. "Well, let's put it like this—you like the Eagles?"

"The band? Yeah, why?"

"So, what's your favorite song by them?"

"I don't know," I said, running their songs through my head. I held up the bottle. "Tequila Sunrise!"

Vek stood, tossed his branch in the fire and walked to the shrubs where he'd come from. "You sure about that, chief?"

Was this some sort of stupid riddle? A philosophical brain teaser? Or was I just drunk, as usual? "Hey, do I know you?" But when I looked up, Vek was gone, along with my bonfire and the beach. I was no longer in Mexico, but standing on my childhood porch, staring into Mom's eyes, attempting to keep my balance as alcohol coursed through my body like a raging river.

"So," she hissed, "you want to be like me, huh? Wanna drink your life away and lose everything you love?"

She walked to the liquor cabinet, pulled out a bottle of dark booze, then came back and stood less than a foot away. My head was spinning, eyes burning, as the alcohol churned away inside my 13-year-old belly.

Mom unscrewed the cap and held out the bottle. "Here, take a drink."

"No," I said, forcefully, nauseous by the mere sight of it.

She held the bottle closer to my face. "Go on…take a nice, long drink."

"No!" I said, pushing the bottle away. The smell made me want to puke.

"What's wrong? Don't you want to be a man? Wait, I know, how 'bout I take a drink?" She put the bottle to her lips.

"No!" I yanked the bottle from her hand before she could drink any. No matter how much I hated her, or pretended to hate her, the last thing I wanted in the world was for her to drink again. I'd been down that path before and had no desire to return. Mom had been sober for two years at that point, and regardless of all the shit she'd put me through over the years, I loved her. It was a complicated love, fraught with pain and distrust and challenges. A love a boy carries for his mother the moment he's connected to her by an umbilical cord. A love which grows and braids and strengthens. A bond that only true evil can break.

"Well, if you can drink, why can't I?" Mom said. "Hey, I have an idea…let's drink together?"

Tears streamed down my face. "Mom, I'm sorry…"

"Go on, drink. I want to see it." She lifted the bottle from the bottom as I held it in my hand, pressing the glass against my face.

"Stop it!" I screamed, pushing the bottle away. Alcohol splashed against my chin and fell to the ground. "I won't ever drink again," I pleaded, wiping tears and snot from my face. "I promise."

She snatched the bottle from my hand. "Go to bed. We'll discuss this tomorrow."

I went inside my room and laid down. But it wasn't until I heard the clanking of glass before I could fully breathe again, knowing that Mom had put the bottle away, returned it to its rightful home—the alchemist's cabinet. Moments later, the room spun. Round and round and round. I spread my arms out and prayed for the ride to end.

I woke up in El Socorro, Tequila bottle in hand. It was early morning, the sky pitch black. The fire had died out, casting a chill over my camp. I shivered. My body was cold. So very cold. And empty. So very empty. I crawled through the sand on my hands and knees, alone and desperate, a tidal wave of despair crashing over me. Then, without warning, all that pent up anger and hurt and sadness erupted, a volcano of pain. I screamed at the top of my lungs, "Motherfucker! Motherfucker! Motherfucker! I'm done. I'm done…I'm fucking done!"

Adrenaline surging, I stood and sprinted toward the ocean, kicking up sand with every step. I reached the water and kept running, pushing through the waves and the tide until the water was up to my waist. Then I stopped and looked toward the sky. The moon shone bright, like it had all those years before. The stars were everywhere, galaxies of hope. I wasn't alone. I was in the universe's cradle. And would be forevermore.

The ocean was cold, lapping against my stomach, but I felt a union with it that was comforting and warm. Reaching out to touch it, I discovered the Tequila bottle was still in my hand. Seren-fuckin-dipity! Destiny was reaching out, and I was going to seize it. I stretched my arm back like a javelin thrower and chucked that fucking bottle as hard and as far as I could. It sailed up into the sky, suspended in time, splashing down a world away. "I'm fucking done," I whispered.

Chapter 14

The winds were swirling as I packed up my gear and prepared for the trip home. The sky turned an ominous shade of gray as I tossed the cooler and beach chair into the van. A storm was brewing. I looked at the ocean. The surf was kicking up, rolling in from the south. But I was heading north, back to Mari, to let her know about everything churning inside my head. I slid my surfboard into the back; the waves continuing to build.

I'd been eyeing a bluff about five to ten miles to the south, thinking it would make a perfect break on a south swell. Now the weather gods were aligning to bring that very swell. My mind was thrown into a conundrum. Go home or go surf? Drink or don't drink? Stay in the U.S. and slowly die, or take off for parts unknown? I'd just drive to the bluff for a look. No harm in that.

The rain danced across my windshield, light at first, a steady pitter patter. But as I neared the bluff, the rain picked up; the skies turning from gray to black. *Just turn around*, I told myself. But I didn't; I just kept on driving, convincing myself I'd only check out the surf, then make a beeline for home. A patch of overgrown scrub brush obscured the turnoff, but I found an opening and pointed the van west.

The dirt road seemed to go on forever. Five miles turned to ten, then ten to fifteen. Visibility dropped, and I wondered if I was steering in the right direction. The VW grunted and snorted, traversing the rugged terrain, powering up and down hills with rain banging down on her roof. I spotted the bluff in the distance and plotted a course.

Rattling up a final embankment, I got a bird's-eye view of the ocean and a cove tucked inside the south side of the hill. A set of waves came charging in, exploding against an outcropping of spires that jutted up from the water like black icebergs. Water spit into the air, then continued on, crashing against the jagged rocks that lined the shore.

I hopped out of the van and paced along the cliff, assessing the situation. Fog rolling in, steady rain, wind picking up—but the surf was still organized. And cranking! Eight feet at least. My heart pounded as I searched for a way to paddle out. Farther up the coast was a black pebble beach, but taking off from it would entail a long, grueling paddle to reach the lineup. Pass!

I wedged myself into my wetsuit, still cold and wet, while staring out at the waves, which were getting heavier by the minute. The rain was coming down diagonally as I grabbed my board and tiptoed along the cliff, searching for a spot to jump. Waves plowed into the rocks. I looked back to my VW, warm and safe. *What if I just went back and watched?*

"Don't be a fucking pussy," was my brain's response.

I looked up and down the beach. Not another living soul for miles. A storm was cracking just offshore. Rocky cliffs. Demon spires. Heavy surf. Fog. A wave came barreling in and before my brain could react, I threw my board into the ocean and jumped in after it.

Surfacing, I grabbed my board and strapped on my leash. The surge was powerful, pulling me toward the cliffs. I paddled harder, pumping my arms and kicking my feet. But the surge kept pulling me back, closer and closer to the rocks. Hearing the waves smash behind me, I kicked and paddled with a fury, duck diving under an avalanche of whitewash. I kept working, pushing myself away from the cliffs. I paddled farther into the ocean, maneuvering around the spires.

When I reached the lineup, the point of safety just past the breaking waves, I laid my head on my board, exhausted and trying to catch my breath. But an enormous wave came barreling in, and I wasn't far enough out to escape it, so I punched and kicked the sea, creeping over the monster and sliding down its back moments before it exploded behind me. A shotgun blast of mist sprayed the back of my neck, sending a shiver down my spine.

What the fuck was I thinking? This was way heavier than I expected. I'd take one wave and one wave only. Surf it toward the black pebble beach. Avoiding the spires, razor blades waiting to slice me up. And the cliffs, which could pulverize my bones into powder.

I sat up on my board and scanned the skies. Dark and angry. A petulant god pounding his fists. The waves continued to grow, reaching the size of small buildings as they stormed past me, churning up the sea and breaking in every direction. The ocean was a battlefield, and I was a soldier. Wind pierced my nostrils and saltwater burned my eyes. Chaos was engulfing me.

I searched for a wave to take me to safety, but they were all so giant. A rip current began pulling me out to sea. I paddled parallel to the shore, but the current was too strong. I pumped my arms and kicked my feet, but my body grew weak. I was no match for its power. I shivered, the icy water turning my head into a popsicle. Through patches of fog, I could see the shore drifting away. *I'm such a fucking idiot.* I could be sitting in my van right now, heater on full blast, making my way back to Mari. Why couldn't I ever just leave well enough alone and accept life for what it is? Why did I always have to push myself?

I turned my head and rested it on my board. The wax felt good against my cheek, comforting somehow. I thought about the hitchhiker I'd picked up just a few days ago. Had he made it to Cabo yet? Sold his guitars? I remembered how, drunk off my ass and careening toward the edge of a cliff, I'd screamed "Don't be a pussy!" Remembered the fear in his eyes as he held the door handle and readied himself to jump.

"Don't be a pussy!" Such an idiotic, childish phrase. A phrase I'd co-opted and spun into a life's mantra. An internal driving force cobbled together by stupidity and hollowness. And for what? What the hell did I have to prove?

The cliffs faded into the fog. *Just disappear, Kev, crawl into the void.* I closed my eyes and let the current take me. I didn't have any fight left. I'd been running so fast, and so far, and for so long—that I just wanted to stop. Wanted to lay my sword down and go to sleep. No more battles. But as I closed my eyes, that stupid mantra came roaring back, drums pounding, stoking the fire inside my belly. *Don't be a pussy! Don't be a pussy!*

I opened my eyes and paddled, pumping my arms to the beat within, pushing through the gray soup, back in the fight. Giant swells glided under my belly, thrusting me into the sky. I moved forward, using the tide as a compass. Exhaustion set in, looking for that knockout blow, my arms like deadweight. But then the bluff appeared, peeking through the fog and the rain. A mixture of adrenaline and hope flooded into my central nervous system. I was back in the lineup, just outside the impact zone, where monsters were waging war.

After catching my breath, I sat up on my board. My body couldn't take much more. I had to get back to shore. But the waves were insane, well over 15-feet now. And stormy, churning in all directions. I'd have to surf in, negotiating the spires and rocky shore. If I fell, I'd be skewered or crushed. I'd catch a wave and ride it to the black pebble beach.

A set of waves rolled in, skyscrapers barreling toward me. I paddled quick and hard over the first two, which exploded like bombs behind me. The third wave was even bigger and scarier. But this was my chance. I had to go.

I spun my board around and got into position. Seconds later, the wave lifted me into the sky. Higher and higher I rose, like a feather in a rush of wind. I paddled and kicked until my momentum allowed me to descend the face of the wave. Then I popped to my feet, digging my toes into the fiberglass. The wave was choppy and angry. It spit out a burst of water and air, shooting me across the wave like a bullet from a gun. Buckets of seawater dumped on my head as I locked my knees and spread out my arms, a statue made of stone.

The ride seemed to last forever. I was in a time warp and wanted to stay. There was no darkness here. No pain. No chaos. Only light and life. Up the coast lay the black pebbly shore. All I had to do was keep riding. But the demon tickled my ear, telling me to ride one more. *Don't be a pussy!* So, against all logic, I rode out the back and paddled back into the storm.

I hadn't gone very far when a tremendous wave crashed in front of me. I tried duck diving, but got sucked down, tumbling and spinning like a ragdoll in a Pitbull's jaws. I surfaced as another wave was crashing in front of me. I took a breath and dove, trying to escape its wrath. The surge snatched my board and dragged us through the water. The leash stretched taut around my ankle, sling-shotting me through the ocean. I tried to rip it off but was somersaulting too fast. When I surfaced, I followed the leash back to the board and climbed on, thankful I hadn't removed it, as the surfboard was my life preserver now.

The cliffs were just a few feet away; the surge pushing me toward them. I tried paddling away from the jagged rocks, but my arms were bone tired. And swimming pools of water kept rushing in. I'd paddle ten feet, dive under a surge of water and be immediately dragged back, trapped in a vicious loop. I paddled harder, envisioning my body being pulverized into a bloody pulp. But my arms felt like wet noodles, and I was too exhausted to make it to the black pebble beach.

I scanned the cliff, searching for the spot I'd jumped. It'd only been a few hours since I made the leap, but it felt like a lifetime ago. A surge of whitewash came rushing in, but instead of fighting it, I let it take me. I was in a horror movie, strapped to a conveyor belt and moving toward a buzz saw. But just as

I was about to smash into the rocks, I flipped my board around and used it as a shield. My knuckles split open as I slid across the rocks, my board sandwiched between me and the cliff.

When the water receded, I ripped off my leash and threw my board. Moments later, a wave crashed against my back. I slid across the crags, ripping my wetsuit and scraping my shoulders and forehead. I dug my fingers into a crevice and held on for dear life, knowing it would be the end of my story if I let go. My surfboard tumbled down the rocks as the water retreated. A lull in the ocean's fury sent me scrambling up the cliff.

Just past the waterline, I stopped to catch my breath. I was bloody and scraped up, but alive! Below me, another monster smashed into the rocks, sending spray thirty feet into the air and dragging my board out to sea. A sacrifice to the gods. I climbed the rest of the way up and laid down in the dirt. Wetsuit shredded and ego bruised. I was exhausted—and had been for 28 years.

Sobriety: Day 1.

Chapter 15

"Mari, Mari," I said, gently touching her shoulder as she slept. But she didn't wake, just kept right on sleeping, indifferent to my absence—now presence. Her face was so peaceful, a million miles from all my bullshit. Floating blissfully in her private world. Free from my sullenness and whining; my disappearing acts and general morose; my sweeping indictment of the world, and how I believed it was completely and utterly fucked up, inherently skewed against me. Yes, here in her dream world, Mari truly was free. Free from the boy who'd taken her from her family, her country, and everything she'd ever known in the world.

"Mari," I repeated, nudging her shoulder, pulling her from her peace and tranquility once more. I'd driven through the night, leaving Mexico behind, to be right here. She opened her eyes and stared into mine. Relief cascaded through her pupils, followed by a wave of anger.

"Don't be mad," I said, hoping to head off the attack. I sat on the edge of the bed and touched her hand. "Mari, I've made a decision…"

She looked on, apprehensive, having seen this movie a hundred times before. I squeezed her hand. "I quit drinking."

She scanned my eyes and studied my voice, searching for downcast pupils and drops in tone. Anomalies in her human polygraph machine. Having already formed a baseline from past declarations of: "I'll cut back," or "I'll only drink on the weekends," to the ever popular, "Just one more."

"Oh, please, you say that all the time." She pushed my hand away, yanked the covers up to her chin, and looked away. It was true, I was a broken record. She'd heard it all before, knew all my tricks. Who could blame her for calling bullshit?

"But this time is different. I really am done. I got it all out of my system. I'm tired of fighting, Mari. Tired of the hangovers. Tired of being tired. I just want to go to Nicaragua with you. But I need you on my side. If we're pulling in different directions, it'll never happen. We need to be a team again."

Her eyes narrowed, calculating, assessing my credibility. Could she trust me, or was this all just a ploy—a new con? But I had a secret, one that would eliminate her doubts. My eyes were sharp and clear, cleansed from the saltwater and tears. My secret was that I truly had quit drinking. There was no ploy or con. No bullshit. No games…

I'd come face to face with my demons in Mexico. That smug son-of-a-bitch who lives inside, constantly pulling me in the wrong direction. The same fucker who'd goaded me into slapping Mari. That inner voice who constantly whispers, "Aw, fuck it, Kev, just have a drink. Don't be such a pussy!"

I faced him that day surfing, as I drifted out to sea, beads of wax caressing my cheek. I knew I wasn't strong enough to take him on. Not directly. At least not yet. So, I devised a plan, a plan to trick him. Knowing we both shared something in common: an all-powerful, unwavering will to survive. You see, without me, there is no him. Now whether there can be a me without him…now that's the real mystery.

So, I paddled, with all my might, alone in that vast ocean, strength waning, fog obscuring my path—fighting to survive. And as my battle hymn kicked in, "Don't be a pussy! Don't be a pussy! Don't be a pussy!" I realized something for the first time, that I could use my negativity as a force. Harness it and allow it to drive me forward instead of always backward.

Perhaps even use it to trick my mind. Convince it not to drink. For today and only today. Tomorrow, I'd play a new trick, and maybe, in time, I'd rack up enough days to put me back in the captain's chair of my life. To make the demon disappear.

"If you ever…" Mari began.

"I won't!"

"If you ever start drinking again, I won't go back to Nicaragua with you. Ever."

"Deal," I said, without hesitation.

The next few weeks flew by. I was true to my word. No drinking. I kept my mind busy studying maps of Mexico and Central America, figuring out optimal routes to maximize my surfing time. I plotted various destinations, constantly drawing and redrawing lines whenever a new, must-see location was discovered. A curvature of land where a hidden surf spot might be, or a desolate strand of coast waiting to be explored. The trip down to Nicaragua would be the ultimate adventure. A combination of surfing, fishing, camping and exploring. I'd be the Magellan of the twentieth century—discovering unknown lands while blazing my trail. I couldn't wait to get on the road. But that day was a long way off.

My mind was in constant motion, keeping the booze demon at bay. If I slowed, even for a minute, he'd work his way back to the helm, dashing all my strength and guile. Then, all it would take is the clinking of two glasses, or the thud of a shot glass being slammed on the bar for him to take control.

So, after a complete and thorough analysis, and plotting my route through Mexico and Central America, I moved onto lists. Lists of every sort. Long, meticulous, highly organized lists. Categorizing every item that a traveler could ever want or need. There were surfboards, of course. A short board for day-to-day surfing. A longboard for small surf. And a medium-sized board, or 'gun,' for big waves.

And speaking of guns, I wondered if I should bring one along as well. A real one, for protection. But I'd never owned a gun before. Never even fired one. Unless you count that time when I was twelve and drove out to the desert with my buddy Mike. His dad let us smoke Camel Non-Filters while popping off soda cans with a .22 rifle, presumedly to teach Mike—and, by extension, me—how to be a man. But the cigarettes made me cough violently, twisting my stomach into knots. And the recoil from the rifle hurt my shoulder, making me hate it with every squeeze of the trigger. I wondered, later, while puking my guts out all over the Borrego Desert, if maybe I was ready to be a man just yet.

Mike got a paper route later that year, his dad wanting to teach him about hard work and the value of a dollar, even though Mike lived in one of the biggest houses in Kensington—an upscale enclave in San Diego which my friends and I referred to as 'Rich-kid Row.' Mike got clipped by a passing car while tossing newspapers onto the porches of other rich kids, his brain swelling inside his skull. He was in the hospital for a long time, nobody knowing whether he'd survive. Thankfully, he pulled through, although I'd lost contact with him by then.

I saw Mike one last time, as he gathered books and other belongings from his locker at Wilson Junior High. He wore a thick batting helmet to protect his head. His dad looked on, a deep sadness in his eyes. My breathing increased as I neared, perhaps a fear of my own mortality. I raised my hand to say hello, or perhaps goodbye, but Mike turned away. He handed his dad the last of his things, closed his locker, and walked away. I never saw Mike again.

I decided not to bring a gun, vowing to brave the world with my own two hands. I turned my attention to more important subjects, such as fishing poles and tackle. Then moved onto books, making individual lists for each genre. I was leaving the U.S. for the rest of my life and needed to be fully stocked and prepared for anything and everything.

Meanwhile, back at work, VP Jim was signing off on loans faster than a man scribbling his name in a hotel register as his hot new girlfriend purrs in his ear. Our bank was on fire, our monthly goals doubling and tripling. The fax machine needed to be refilled every hour on the hour to keep up with demand. We wrote so many checks that we had to order a larger safe to hold them all. Blank checks wheeled in by the pallet. It was a bonanza.

Approved! Approved! Approved!

I watched the checks being printed: two, three, four, five-hundred-thousand dollars, wondering if anybody would notice twenty thousand dollars going missing. A measly twenty thousand dollars. Because that was our goal. To save twenty-grand. And once we had it in the bank, it was GO time. How easy it would've been to type out 'Kevin Cromley' and hit print. I'd be deep in Mexico by the time the check made its way back to the corporate office where it would most likely get lumped in with all the other thousands upon thousands of checks. But I wasn't a thief and wanted to leave the country in good standing.

A cornucopia of neon liquor signs greeted me each night as I drove away from my glass-and-wood prison. Beacons on every corner. But I stared straight ahead, ignoring their bright light. Another day of pushing out loans like a drug dealer selling smack ticking by. But when I hit traffic, and the slog of life set in, I became thirsty. So very thirsty. Taillights mocked me. Oh, how they mocked me. Legions of taillights. Rivers of taillights—meandering endlessly, reminding me of my bottomless thirst and my inability to escape my very skin. I cranked up Black Flag, inviting them to scream into my ears. Anything to drown out that little fucker in my head who kept whispering, "C'mon, Kev, just a wee lil' nip," in some stupid fucking leprechaun accent.

I returned to my lists, mental lists to drown out the chaos. Tools. I would need tools. Let's see, a hammer, of course. Or rather, *hammers.* A roofing hammer for big jobs, a day-to-day hammer, and a small hammer for light work and crafts. I'd need several types of flashlights, starting with the ever-reliable Maglite, the long one, which uses 6 D-batteries. I might not have a gun on this trip, but a solid Maglite would do in a pinch. Now, which color should I go with, blue or black? Blue, so I can spot it in the dark. Actually, let's make it black in case I need to go all Ninja. I'd also need a headlamp for setting up camp at night and exploring in the dark.

The next thing I knew, I was pulling up to our apartment. Another day in the books. One step closer to Nicaragua, and one step further from my last drink. And so, life progressed, putting people in doublewides by day, plotting our escape by night. But, at a certain point, the pace became too much. My mind was exhausted from trying to outrun my demon. I realized I had to slow down, learn to live within the fog as I was in a marathon, not an all-out sprint. I needed to learn how to jog, fast enough to trick my brain, but not so fast that I wore out and gave in to my impulses.

Mari came around slowly, her trust ebbing and flowing. But she was right there by my side as we scoured garage sales and swap meets, looking for kitchen items and camping gear. We were a team again, with a common goal, and our relationship improved. Sobriety was a tulip opening to the sun, warming my spirit and allowing happiness to seep inside. No longer was I edgy and pissed off at the world, but calm and present. I'd been drinking alcohol pretty consistently since high school, and even before that, in middle school, had smoked pot every day. A twisted mess I surely was. Broken. Humpty-fuckin'-Dumpty. Could I put the pieces back together?

By month six, I was going stir crazy. I wanted to leave. To break free. To put my foot on the pedal and drive south. But my finances were in a rut, stuck in first gear. Saving twenty-grand had proved elusive, a hopeless dream. So, I scaled it back. Fifteen thousand was the new number. And once we hit it, we were free to leave. Fifteen thousand to carry us through for the rest of our lives.

But even socking away that much seemed like an impossibility, especially after paying our rent and bills. There was only so much left over at the end of each month. We stopped eating out. Mari never liked greasy burgers to begin with and thought Mexican food was too spicy. We also ceased all the mindless shopping. How many clothes does one person really need? We even stopped going out to the movies, a personal sacrifice, as I loved the escape from reality.

Yet, still, the money wasn't stacking up. There was only one option left. So, with a pang in my side, I picked up the phone.

"You want to *what*?" Mom asked.

"Move in with you," I repeated.

"You've got to be shitting me."

"No, I'm serious. I need this, Mom." I told her about our plans to move back to Nicaragua. About our financial situation, and how I'd felt like an animal trapped in a cage ever since returning from the Peace Corps.

She was quiet for a moment. Almost too quiet. Before finally relenting. "Okay, Kevin…"

Chapter 16

I tossed a Truck Trader on the counter of our local liquor store. The old man behind the counter peered up. "Is that all?" he asked, eager to turn around and grab my usual bottle of rum from the back shelf.

"Yeah, that's it," I replied, a steely resolve nicked into my vocal cords. My eyes stared straight ahead. A horse with blinders. Broken. Each day a steady climb, fighting internal enemies, keeping alcohol at bay. My body healing, my brain un-embalming. Unpickling. Arising from the dead.

Our little nest egg had grown since moving in with Mom, and it was time to make our first purchase. I wanted a Ford truck with a cab-over camper, the kind that sits in the truck's bed. The campers came fully equipped with a toilet, shower and even a stove—a veritable hotel on wheels. My VW van was great for short trips, but it lacked a bathroom and most of the other amenities. It also had zero power. There was no way in hell I was going to putt-putt all the way to Nicaragua in it.

Flipping through the pages, I spotted the perfect truck: A Ford F-250, 6.9-liter diesel engine with heavy duty suspension and two gas tanks. I bought it that very day for $2,500, then immediately put my van up for sale. A teenager showed up a few days later with his mom to have a look. I pointed out all her dings and flaws, before revealing all the love we'd put into her: reupholstered seat cushions, freshly stained wood, and the new curtains Mari had sewn by hand.

The kid was so excited he forgot to talk me down off my $1,400 price. But it was bittersweet watching him drive away, like losing a friend. The van had been part of my life both before and after the Peace Corps, through good times and bad. As the VW motored down Adams Avenue, I took solace in knowing she was in good hands and going to the next generation, soon to be making fresh memories and setting off on new adventures. But it was time to move on, to begin a new chapter of my life. Mari's and my life. Where the road would take us, one could only guess. Yet the prospects were boundless.

I found the cab-over camper in nearby El Cajon. After telling the owner about our trip, he agreed to knock off $300 from his asking price of $1200. It took about an hour for him to walk me through all the different features and systems on the camper, including the pump and sewer system, the propane gas setup, the fresh-water reservoirs, and the jacks that raised it on and off the truck bed. As I was leaving, he mentioned he had a box-style trailer for sale for only $200. I told him I'd think it over and let him know when I came back for the camper the following weekend.

It appeared the plan was finally coming together, the dream within our grasp. I'd been rushing down this path for so long, and so fast, that I'd barely had time to reflect on the new life we were about to embark upon. Now reality was approaching like a runaway freight train. This was happening. There were no brakes, no offramps. I was leaving my life, my family, my country— forever. We had the truck and camper and all the crap we could need. I checked the bank account one last time: $12,000. And I'd be receiving a final paycheck in the two-thousand-dollar range. Fourteen grand. Fuck it—close enough!

"I'm giving my two-week notice."

VP Jim nearly fell out of his chair. "You're what?" He stood and walked toward me; a concerned fatherly-look on his face. But I knew the true concern was for himself, realizing his trained monkey would no longer be around to push out loans at mach-10 speed. There was no need for alarm, however, as I was sure he'd have a fresh donkey in my seat in a matter of weeks.

I wished him well and meant it. Jim was a decent guy, caught up in the system like the rest of us. He worked hard and just wanted to provide for his family. He didn't build the financial web entangling all those who neared. He was just another strand of thread within it. Just interlaced fibers forming a mesh. The only difference: I'd found a way out of the trap.

My last day of work arrived. I muttered a few uncomfortable goodbyes to people I barely knew, even though I'd worked with them for over two years. Then I left my little glass prison overlooking the lush golf course. The sun glared in my eyes as I marched toward the big F-250 truck, aptly named 'The Beast.' A light breeze blew in from the west, rustling the leaves on the nearby trees. It felt like I was in the closing scene of a movie, the hero riding off into the sunset.

"More books?" Mari asked, as I loaded yet another stack of classic and how-to books inside the new trailer. I ended up buying it when I went back for the camper, figuring we could load most of our possessions inside it, keeping the camper clutter free. Nobody wants to be pushing boxes out of their way every time they need to use the restroom or prepare a meal.

The camper was like a miniature house on wheels. It had a small bathroom—tiny really, you could barely turn around in it—with an even smaller shower; a kitchenette, comprising a two-burner propane stove, a sink with water supplied by a two-hundred-gallon fresh-water tank, and a fold-down table with two bench seats. A ladder near the back led to a full-size bed directly above the truck's cab, where a mere twenty inches separated the bed from the ceiling, making for a tight fit and a future filled with bumped heads.

The entire camper fit inside the bed of the truck. The sides resting atop the rails and the front (where the bed was) hanging over the cab. Four clamps secured the camper to the truck. And while the owner had assured me the clamps were strong enough to carry us all the way through Mexico and Central America—I had my doubts. But I was eager to get on the road, ready to start our new adventure. So, I pushed those doubts aside.

I snuck a few more stacks of books inside the trailer as Mari tidied up the camper. The trailer—and when I say *trailer*, I'm referring to a wooden box (4-feet wide, by 4-feet high, by 6-feet long) sitting atop a steel frame, basically a crate on wheels—was relatively small compared to the camper. A door in the rear contained a metal latch secured by a padlock to safeguard our valuables—items we'd collected from garage sales and swap meets. A hodgepodge of 'stuff' we'd collected over the past few months. In fact, if one were to inspect our 'collection,' they might assume we were moving to Nicaragua to open a junkyard, or perhaps even a library. But I was undeterred, knowing I couldn't just pop down to the local library to check out Anna Karenina or Moby Dick. No, I had to bring those books, along with all the others.

The trailer's suspension creaked and moaned as I put the last of the tools, screws, nails, high school yearbooks and old wrestling trophies inside. The entirety of our lives was now packed snugly inside the rectangular box. Mari rolled her eyes as I hummed Beethoven's 5th while closing and locking the door.

Our grand plan had reached its apex. The only thing left was to drive off. To begin our new life. A life where we and we alone controlled our destiny.

No longer subjected to the whims of others. No, we were free, unmoored ships adrift in the vast sea. Explorers. Soon to be camping on far-flung beaches, surfing undiscovered waves…Fishing in secret ponds.

I felt like a boy at a baseball game, opening his hotdog wrapper while big-league ballplayers sprinted out to the field. Patting damp sand into turrets on a sandcastle, sun warm on my cheeks, saltwater lapping at my toes; I felt like a boy with infinite possibilities, with dreams that knew no limits—whose heart held no boundaries. Mostly, I just felt joy. Joy that I was starting life afresh. Who knows, maybe I'd even reconnect—have a chat—with that boy again. A kick-ass kid I'd been pushing away for years.

Mom came outside to see us off, giving Mari a giant hug filled with love and strength. The same love she'd shown me, haphazardly, over the years. A powerful love that shaped me into the man I was. Or the man I was becoming.

"Take care of her," Mom said, as I kissed her on the cheek. "There's few like her."

"I will."

I walked around the truck and trailer one last time, checking the doors and locks, making sure everything was a go. Then I hopped into the cab, put on my shades and pointed the Beast south, toward the San Ysidro Port of Entry—the gateway to Mexico. Mari squeezed my hand as I hit the gas. I smiled, shooting her a look of confidence as the big diesel engine picked up speed. Our rig was solid and strong, like us. It was time to kick some ass. Time to live!

We barreled down the 805 Freeway, determined to cross the border and continue our journey along the rugged and desolate Baja Peninsula, with mountains to our east and the Pacific Ocean to our west. When we reached the southern tip of Baja, we'd camp out for a week or two, then ferry over to mainland Mexico, where we'd continue heading south, hugging the Pacific all the way to Guatemala—a route I'd meticulously plotted over the prior year. Ours would be a life of vagabonds, gypsies crossing the Americas.

Less than twenty minutes later, we reached the border. I slowed and got into the entry line for Mexico. Tijuana lay just ahead, perched on the hills beyond, a busy metropolis of enterprising and hard-working men and women, descendants of the mighty Aztec Empire. Soon, we'd be motoring through it as we worked our way to the coast. "Here we go," I said, flashing a big smile at Mari. She gave a nervous smile in return as we weaved through a series of orange pylons and cement barriers. We arrived at a sign that read 'Welcome to

Mexico,' and proceeded through an inspection station. A light turned red, prompting an agent to flag us down.

"*Hola*," I said with a fake smile.

He didn't return my smile, just took a long look at our rig before asking, "*¿Qué hay en el tráiler?*"

"Oh, just our personal items," I replied. "We're moving to Nicaragua."

He didn't appear at all excited for our new life. And after taking a slow walk around the truck and trailer, he returned to my window. "You can't enter Mexico here. *Ustedes son transportistas*. You must go to the border east of here."

"Wait...I have to go *where*?" I grabbed my passport and held it up. "No, look, I have a Visa. I'm a tourist. It's all right here."

"No, you're not a tourist, and you need to go to the next border. Now, hurry up and turn around. Right up there." I followed his finger, pointing to an area just ahead where we could make a U-turn and reenter the U.S.

"Wait, wait, wait," I pleaded. "Maybe there's some miscommunication going on here." I looked at Mari for some help. My Spanish was pretty decent, so I wasn't quite sure why he wasn't understanding me. Mari talked to him briefly, but he only reiterated what he'd just told me: that we were *transportistas* and needed to enter Mexico from a different border.

"Come on, man, can't you just let us through?"

"No, now turn around before I fine you," he said, waving us off.

I threw my hands up in disgust. "Fuck it, we'll just go to Otay." Driving away, I tried to remember how to get to Otay Mesa, the other border crossing twenty minutes to the east. I noticed an old man sitting on a stool in front of an outdoor food stand. He wore a straw hat and was drinking a beer. But not just any beer, a Dos Equis, the one in the green bottle. The same beer I used to drink when I traveled through Mexico. I could even see the condensation on the neck of the bottle, mini rivulets of water. My body turned instantly clammy, and my salivary glands began pumping out buckets of spit. I made the U-turn and headed back to the U.S., the muscles in my shoulders tightening. *Just relax, Kev, you'll be in Mexico before you know it.*

I'd been sober for six months, not a drop of the devil juice. Mari had been hesitant in the beginning, waiting for me to slip and return to my old ways. Listening for the slam of the front door after every fight or argument, the signal I was racing up to the liquor store. But I never did, just kept pushing those little demon fuckers away, rowing with all my might, keeping far away from their treacherous shoals. And as the days passed, so too did the urges. Slightly at first, but enough to give me hope. Hope there could be an escape, light at the end of the metaphorical tunnel.

A gust of air whipped up the map as I pressed it against the steering wheel. Mari held the corners down while I searched for a route through Tijuana. This was all just a minor hiccup. Mari smiled, her lips the color of a plum. She'd stuck by me through a lot of shit, even when I was wading up to my eyeballs in it with no hope of escape. Even though she never said it, I think it disappointed her that we hadn't 'conquered' America. Hadn't 'made' it. But we'd extracted from it what we needed, saving a whopping $14,000, which we would use to start a business once we arrived in Nicaragua. Our options were unlimited. Mari touched my shoulder and pointed to the Otay Mesa Point of Entry.

"No, you can't cross here," said a Mexican border agent, flipping through our passports. His uniform was creased to perfection, and he wore the same Aviator sunglasses as the agent in San Ysidro. I wondered if they were standard issued. "*Ustedes son transportistas*," he said with a scowl. "You have to cross in Texas."

"Texas!" I yanked my non-Aviator sunglasses from my face and chucked them across the cab. "Are you fucking serious? First of all, I'm not a *transportista*—whatever the hell that is. And second, why the hell would I go to Texas? That's just ridiculous. Now, where's your boss?"

"Calm down," Mari said in a low voice, grabbing my sunglasses off the floorboard and setting them on my leg. But as my face grew redder and my voice louder, she realized there was no calming me down and slid across the cab toward the window.

"I *am* the boss," said the agent in a calm, direct manner. "You can't enter Mexico here. You need to go to the east."

"Wait a minute," I took a deep breath, trying to rein in my anger. "Look, I'm sorry, I'm just a little upset. We've been planning this trip for over a year, and I just don't understand why we can't enter here. I've been visiting Mexico since I was a kid and never had a problem like this before."

"I'm sorry," he said, handing back our passports. "You have a transit visa, not a tourist visa. You say you're moving to Nicaragua and have a trailer full of belongings, which means you're a *transportista.* Therefore, you can only enter Mexico from certain ports of entry."

"Okay, fine, but there has to be another port of entry besides Texas? I mean, that doesn't sound right at all, that I'd have to travel all that way."

"You could try Arizona, but for right now, you need to turn around and proceed back to the U.S."

I put my now crooked shades back on my face and punched the gas. There was no point arguing with the agent any longer. It would not change the fact that, after all the hours spent carefully planning and researching every possible route to Nicaragua, I'd fucked up on the most basic of tasks—entering Mexico. Granted, I was an idiot, but there was no way in hell I was driving all the way across Texas. That would destroy my plans. No, I could salvage this thing.

So, after flipping a quick U-turn—I was becoming rather adept at spinning our rig from Mexico to America—I headed north for twenty minutes until I hit the 8, then turned east, away from my beloved ocean, my blood pressure rising with each mile that ticked away on the odometer. After several miles of anger bubbling up inside, I pulled over before I erupted altogether. Snatching the map off the dashboard, I spread it out, staring at all the perfectly analyzed, hypothesized, scrutinized, theorized, plotted lines. But as the San Diego sunshine illuminated the pages, I realized that all my painstaking cartographic work—all those perfectly etched lines—were all meaningless now.

"Fuck Baja! We'll just work our way over to Arizona, then drop into mainland Mexico near the Sea of Cortez. We can travel across the mountains to the Pacific. Besides, the Sea of Cortez is amazing, best fishing in the world. And the fish tacos are out of this world!" Mari gave me an awkward smile as I attempted to pump myself up. This wasn't a setback. No, not at all. It was all part of our new way of life, of going with the flow and not letting obstacles bring us down. A detour, which would only enhance our experience.

I cranked up Yellowman as the Beast climbed the Peninsular Range, swaying my shoulders to the reggae beat. *No worries, mon.* We rolled across Ocotillo Wells, soaking up the desert's tranquility and serenity. Yet somewhere amidst the dunes and bluffs, I decided—always obstinate—to try and enter Mexico via California one last time, this time via Mexicali. We were rebuffed, once again, by a border agent even more serious than the previous two, wearing the trademark Aviators and in no mood to argue with the gringo. He told me, in no uncertain terms, that I needed to go to Texas to enter Mexico.

Furious by all the setbacks but determined to make it into Mexico by day's end, I motored on, not giving the agent any heed. Even Mari was growing frustrated by our predicament. It was well past three in the afternoon when we pulled up to the border in Nogales, Arizona, both of us on pins and needles as we watched the Mexican agent approach our window. "*¿Pasaportes?*"

I handed them over and waited, nervously flicking the corner of our map as he scrolled through the pages, stopping when he found our visa. He looked up from the passports and scanned the camper, his eyes settling on the trailer. I wanted to jump out and unhook that motherfucker right then and there. Donate it, along with the thousand pounds of books inside, to the Mexican Immigration and Customs Division. But before I could put my plan in motion, the agent's lips formed and then enunciated the words I now knew by heart: "You are a *transportista* and need to…"

I tuned him out after '*transportista*,' the air leaving my body like a deflated balloon. Oddly, even though I'd been summarily rejected for the umpteenth time, I felt a sense of relief come over me. A resignation to the fact that my entire year of planning was now officially kaput. Over. *No más*. It was time to start over. To make new plans. To re-analyze, re-hypothesize, re-scrutinize, re-theorize, re-plot. Time to say, "Fuck it!"

My dream of traveling down the Pacific Coast of Mexico, of surfing empty waves and sleeping on remote, uninhabited beaches, was dissolving before my very eyes. Dropping into Mexico from Texas would completely obliterate that dream, forcing me to travel around the Gulf of Mexico, where waves were almost nonexistent. It seemed cruel, like waving a bottle of water in front of a man dying of thirst.

I felt the old anger rise, that molten lava that sat just below the surface. I was angry with our situation, angry with my stupidity. "Why can't we just enter Mexico from Texas?" Mari asked, her tone full of hope and enthusiasm. She appeared so young. Her skin soft, eyes eager, pushing my anger down, driving the magma back inside my gut. Back into my intestines and my bowels. Cactus shot by as we crossed the desert, heading farther away from the ocean. Further away from my dreams.

My eyes bounced from the sand and cactus to Mari. Her smile made the world more complete, made life and all its flaws infinitely more interesting, made my fleeting dreams of the Pacific Ocean bearable. But I had a secret: Puerto Angel and Puerto Escondido. Two small towns in the southern Mexico state of Oaxaca, where our road would meet back up with the Pacific Ocean after traveling the breadth and width of Mexico. Two spots where the surf absolutely rips under the right conditions. "We can, mi amor…We can…" I told Mari, as the sky turned purple, and the sun dipped below the horizon.

Chapter 17

We pulled into a rest stop somewhere in New Mexico. We figured if they would not let us into Mexico, we'd at least test out the camper. As you entered the rear door, there was a bathroom immediately to your left, and the kitchen to the right. Just beyond the loo, was a foldup table with two bench seats, where I spread out our well-worn map, letting the edges hang over the sides. Mari lit a match and turned on the two-burner stove, heating up some leftover rice and chicken—remnants from a previous life.

"That agent said we had to go all the way to Brownsville, which is near the Gulf of Mexico. Basically, the end of Texas. I'm thinking we should try a different border, a closer one. What do you think?"

Mari continued stirring the food, unfazed by my question, indifferent to my self-created dilemma. I viewed Mexico as the starting point to our new life—our new adventure—and driving clear across Texas would delay that start even longer. But I was also sick and tired of being turned back at every border crossing from San Diego to wherever the hell I was. I stared at the map, studying all the different routes from Texas to Nicaragua. Driving across Texas to the Gulf of Mexico had one advantage: it meant we'd be staying on well-paved U.S. highways for a sizable portion of the trip. And when we crossed into Mexico—assuming that ever happened—we could follow the much shorter route along the Gulf of Mexico, through Veracruz, then over the Oaxaca Mountains to the Pacific. The Pacific!

After dinner, we crawled up the ladder and sunk into bed. It was tight up there, the ceiling just a few inches from our face. You couldn't sit up, and if you wanted to rollover, you had to scoot around incrementally, always careful not to whack your head. When we finally got ourselves comfortable, I wrapped my arms tight around Mari and let the world disappear. Men in Aviator glasses, borders, maps…doubt and uncertainty—all faded away. Here, in this little nook of the world, we were safe and content.

We were back on the road at the crack of dawn, barreling across the flat, dusty highways of Texas, yellow grass and dirt as far as the eye could see. The state seemed to go on forever. We drove and drove, stopping only to refuel. The Beast's 6.9-liter engine burned through a lot of diesel. The two tanks had been a godsend, eliminating the need to fill up every hour on the hour. Mari pointed out a caravan of tractor trailers. The line seemed to go on forever. Mixed in with the pack was an odd assortment of compact cars towing other compact cars, Japanese mostly. Our little parade was all heading in the same direction. East.

My curiosity won out and at the next gas station, I asked a short Latino guy pumping gas into a Toyota Corolla towing another Toyota Corolla where he and all the other cars like him were heading. He looked on confused, so I switched to Spanish.

"*Vamos a Matamoros* to cross the border," he said.

"Oh, we're driving to the border, too. Are you from Mexico?"

"No, El Salvador," he replied.

I continued my little investigation, discovering that these enterprising men came up to the U.S. every month to buy cheap, four-cylinder cars, connecting them together with rods and chains, then driving them all the way back down to Honduras and El Salvador to sell them at a profit. A whole cottage industry that few Americans knew about.

"So, where is Matamoros?" I asked.

"On the border of Mexico and Brownsville, Texas."

"Why do you have to go all the way there?"

"Because we're *transportistas*," he replied.

I almost shit myself. There it was, that stupid fucking name again. And then it all became clear. We were being lumped in with these guys, with the car-towing-other-car guys, and the semi-trucks, and all the other commercial enterprises and transporters. Even though the only thing we were transporting was a thousand pounds of books and some old, rusty tools. I should've listened to Mari from the beginning, when she told me not to bring all that junk. That we wouldn't need it. I thought about unhooking the trailer and ditching it at the next rest stop. A donation to the local library, a donation for the local dump. But we'd gone too far by then, and there was no turning back. No, the trailer would stay. But I took a measure of solace, knowing we were finally heading in the right direction. To the end of the world…the end of Texas.

We spent the night at another rest stop, then hit the road early and hard the next day, opening up the beast and letting her roar across Texas. We were on a mission, bypassing the famed barbecue joints and ranch towns that seemed to spring up out of nowhere, then quickly fade into the yellow grass. The land went on forever.

When we finally pulled into Brownsville, our hearts were racing. We'd made it. We found the border entry and made our way through the line. But after crossing into Mexico, yet another Mexican agent immediately flagged us down. He wasn't wearing Aviators, but a pissed off scowl, letting us know straight away that he didn't take any shit. "Go back to Reynosa," he said curtly.

"Reynosa…Where's that?" I asked, my stomach now in my throat.

He pointed west, the same direction we'd just come from. I nearly died, right there in Matamoros or Brownsville or wherever the fuck I was. I'd been driving for two days straight and told a different story at every border. Now, this cat was telling me to turn around and head back west. What the hell! I closed my eyes and breathed. There was no sense arguing, especially with this guy who seemed about as serious as a heart attack. I turned our little rig around and drove back into the U.S. while Mari opened up the map and searched for Reynosa. It took every ounce of willpower to not punch the ceiling 500 times.

Thankfully, Reynosa was only about an hour away. But Reynosa is in Mexico, so we headed to McAllen, the Texas city that straddles it. When we arrived, it appeared as if every semi and big rig in the in the world was there, lined up miles deep, along with hundreds of the cars-towing-other-cars dudes. We were definitely at the right spot.

McAllen was a bustling city of commerce. A large sector devoted to truckers and commercial vehicles. Everywhere you looked were commercial vehicles. Tractor trailers, heavy equipment, tow trucks, some pulling other semis, flatbeds carrying giant spools of wire, factory equipment or massive electrical components. But the one thing I didn't see were other RVs and campers like ours. It pissed me off we were being lumped in with this class of vehicles.

I pulled into a dirt lot where a group of truckers were standing around shooting the shit. I asked if they were driving into Mexico, and where we were supposed to go to enter the line. The men, all speaking Spanish, were friendly and eager to help. They pointed to a column of trucks that seemed to go from one end of McAllen to the other. "*Allá* está *la línea*-That's the line."

"That line there? Holy shit!" A bead of sweat dripped down my scalp and rolled across my nose. "Isn't there a shorter line for vehicles like mine?"

"It's all the same line," said one man. I nearly shit a brick, right there in Texas as I contemplated the longest line in America, the heat pushing ninety and rising. And for one moment, I contemplated turning the Beast around and heading straight back to San Diego, extricating myself from this insidious clusterfuck I'd found myself in. But before I could find a wall to slam my head into, a young man wearing an official-looking vest and an ID badge on a lanyard approached us. "Excuse me, sir, do you have your manifest and border entry documents?"

"Who are you?" I asked, trying to figure out just who in the hell this guy was. I was still on the U.S. side, after all. Or at least I thought I was. Hell, I could have been in Canada for all I knew. I was so confused.

"I'm a *transportista* agent," he said, flashing his lanyard ID. "And I can file your paperwork." He pointed to an office in the lot's corner.

"You're a *what*? No, no, no, I don't need any *transportista* documents. I already have my visa. But thanks anyway."

"Yes, you have your visa, but do you have your manifest and entry documents?"

I felt a scam coming on—but was having a hard time figuring it out. Was lanyard boy a legit official? And if so, for what agency? He was definitely not from U.S. Customs and Borders Protection. But maybe he worked for some third-party contractor that expedited entry into Mexico for commercial vehicles. I just couldn't understand how, while still in the U.S., I could be so completely lost. I opened my passport and flashed him my Mexican visa. "See? All neatly stamped and official."

"No, that's your visa. But you are in transit. Look, it's written right there in your passport. You still need a manifest and all your entry documents. But don't worry, I can do it all for you. And for only $800."

I burst out laughing. Riddle solved. This guy was trying to scam me. What kind of idiot did he take me for? "No way, bro. Go away, I don't need you."

"Okay, sir, but our office is right over there if you change your mind." He pointed to the office and walked away.

"Can you believe that little fucker?" I asked Mari. She just shrugged. Nothing made sense anymore. I decided to double check with a few of the other truckers before I got into the mile-long line. *"Esa es la línea para entrar Mexico?"*

"Si, si," they confirmed. "That's the right line to enter Mexico."

"Okay, gracias." I turned and headed back to the truck. But a few steps later, I stopped and turned around. "Oh, and one last thing, what's up with these manifest and *transportista* documents? Do I really need those?"

They smiled and held up fistfuls of papers. "Yes, everybody must have them to enter Mexico."

I felt a pang in my stomach, like I'd eaten a bad batch of oysters. "Aw, shit, really? And they cost $800?"

"Yes, and you can't get into Mexico without them. But you can probably get them for less than $800."

Our budget was tight, with no room for unexpected costs. Mari and I trudged to the office, where we found the young guy inside with a smile from ear to ear. "So, are you ready now?"

"Yes," I said, "but I'm not paying $800. I'll give you $100."

"No, that's impossible. There is a lot of work involved. The least I could do it for is $400."

"Bro, I'm moving to Nicaragua to live for the rest of my life. I don't have $800 or even $400. Can't you just hook me up? It's not like I'm one of those big semi-trucks hauling a full load of merchandise. I just have a camper and a little trailer."

"Well, what exactly are you transporting?"

"I'm not transporting anything. I'm bringing some random household items, like tools and dishes…and books. Lot of books." I glanced sideways, wondering if Mari was staring daggers into my neck.

I haggled with him for a few minutes before settling on a price of $250. After ponying up the cash, he set about filling out an endless array of forms and documents. Once they were all complete, he passed them off to an older lady with a sweet smile who banged away on a typewriter from the 1800s, while lanyard boy took us outside to inspect the truck and trailer. He wrote the year, make, model, color, Vin, and license plate number of the truck, and then asked me to open the trailer.

After unlocking the Master Lock and pulling back the wooden door, a musty odor wafted out. The smell of rust and decaying cardboard from old boxes and plastic containers filled with junk packed into every square inch of the trailer.

"*Ay, señor*…what's in all those boxes?"

"I told you already. Tools and books…and other assorted items."

"Well, we need to open them. All of them. And write exactly what's inside each box on the manifest."

"Are you serious? That'll take forever. I told you, it's just a bunch of worthless shit."

"I know, I know, but it's required."

I reached in and pulled out the first box. It was full of old hinges, dusty tape measures, rulers, and other crap you might find in your grandfather's garage. It was official—I was a hoarder. And not just any type of hoarder…but a traveling hoarder. Toting my garbage—my shit—across the globe. My shame grew with every box that was opened, listening as the agent read aloud, then scribbled the name of each piece of junk into his precious manifest. I wished I was a turtle, so that I could tuck my head into my shell and disappear. Mari's face turned redder than mine, as she opened up boxes of napkins I'd nabbed from McDonalds, spools of green and purple thread, broken fishing poles, and raggedy old sheets and blankets that didn't even match.

It got even worse when we hit the motherlode of books. Box upon box of old musty paperbacks and squishy hardbacks. "Why did you have to bring all those books?" Mari asked. "You act as though Nicaragua is in the Middle Ages. We have books there, you know. And bookstores, too. We don't even need this stupid trailer!" Mari's anger was less about books, and more about how I viewed Nicaragua. As if my books were a sweeping indictment of the country. But they weren't. I loved Nicaragua. I just had this video playing out in my head, of surfing all morning, then lying in a hammock and reading all day. Scenes that had helped me survive my two years of working the eight to five grind, of driving through traffic every morning and every night, of dealing with VP Jim and doling out loans to anybody who applied. That was my dream, and that's what those books represented to me. Nothing more and nothing less.

Three hours later, we had the all-important, ever-elusive manifest clenched in our fists, along with another stack of official-looking papers. We were finally ready to cross the border. Finally, ready to embark on our grand adventure. Lanyard boy gave Mari a hug as they'd become friends over the previous few hours, then he shook my hand awkwardly and wished us well in

Nicaragua. Mari and I climbed back inside the Beast and turned on the engine. But just as I was about to put her in gear and drive away, the guy jumped onto our hood and slid up to the windshield.

"What the fu…" Before I could complete my curse word, he unfurled a tube of paper with ten-inch-high letters and affixed it to our windshield. T-R-A-N-S…I looked at Mari, my mouth agape, as her new buddy continued to plaster the oversized letters to the glass. P-O-R-T-I-S-T-A. When he finished, he rubbed all the letters down with his thumb, gave a last wave and smile, then hopped off the truck and disappeared.

It was official; the sticker proved it—our giant scarlet-fucking letter bore witness, erasing all lingering doubts—we were, and would continue to be, *transportistas*. Little did I know just how consequential that label would be to our future. A giant neon sign. A beacon to every cop, sheriff, *federale* and soldier in Mexico. A signal to pull us over and shake us down.

A little over two years prior, I'd reached the lowest point of my life, having just smacked my bride of two months, empty rum bottle between my thighs, drunk off my ass and jonesing for more. I'd reached a juncture, a crossroads of sorts. One path led to darkness. The other, well…that has yet to be determined. Presently, it had led us to this point of embarkation, about to set off on the journey of a lifetime, a demarcation line from our old lives to our new lives. I was only 28 but already exhausted, burned out with the world and my fellow man, teetering on the icy edge of sobriety. Life had been kicking my ass for a while. But, at that moment, I felt like Rocky Balboa charging up those stairs…on top of the world…like a motherfuckin' king.

We drove up the street and found a spot in the mile-long border line, semi-trucks as far as the eye could see. The sun disappeared as we waited and after an hour of stagnation, I finally got out of the truck and walked around. I poked around the semi in front of us but didn't find anybody inside. Walking back to the truck, I spotted the driver lying in a hammock underneath the cargo container, just a few inches off the ground.

"*Hola, amigo*, do you know why we aren't moving?"

"*Están cerrados, abren a las cuatro de la mañana.*"
"*Gracias.*"

I let Mari know they were closed until four the next morning. We climbed into our rooftop bed, our safe little cocoon, and made love. It would be our last night in the U.S. for a long time.

We awoke with a startle. A tremendous roar permeated the camper, a grumbling that shook us to our bones. Looking out the window, the headlights of a thousand trucks instantly blinded me, all revving their big diesel engines as they prepared to cross the border. 4 a.m. had arrived. Time to move.

We hurried out of the camper and into the truck, cranking over the engine. She fired right up, roaring in unison with the other thousands of diesel engines, all eager to make their pilgrimages into Mexico. Luck was on our side as we inched our way to the border. Mari smiled, sleep clinging to the corners of her eyes. An hour later, we crossed into Mexico. And, as usual, were immediately flagged down by a Mexican agent, Aviator glasses tucked inside his shirt pocket.

"Papeles?" he asked, his eyes scanning the truck, stopping on the 'Transportista' sticker spread out across the windshield. *Oh, shit, here we go.* I handed him our passports along with our newly purchased ream of documents—including the precious manifest. He flipped through the papers quickly, then took a slow walk around our rig. I was fiddling with my fingers when he returned to my window, anticipating the words of rejection I knew so well, the directive to turn around and return to the United States. Perhaps he'd tell us to go west this time, back to Arizona. Or farther east, back to the Gulf of Mexico. I waited for his hand to rise and point to the area where I should make my U-turn. Instead, he took a last look at the decal on our windshield, handed back our paperwork, and then waved us through. *¡Bienvenidos a México!*

Chapter 18

Each time I arrive in Mexico, it's as if I've walked through C.S. Lewis's magical wardrobe, a portal into another realm. That first whiff of diesel fuel and burning wood, of tortillas being charred over open flames, sides of pork sweating out their fat as they twirl around rotisseries—smells that transport me back in time to my twelve-year-old self, meandering along the shoreline at Puerto Nuevo, scouring the sand for seashells and colored rocks with my best friend, Trout.

Our hands clinging tight to plastic bags filled with treasure: purple cylindrical shells we use as fake daggers; sand dollars as big as our hands bleached white from the sun, which we will attempt to make necklaces from one day, only to have them crumble and return to sand; and miniature conch shells, prized above all else for their ability to reproduce the sounds of the ocean.

These shells will find their way back to our bedrooms, to rest upon dressers and nightstands. And one day, perhaps months later, we'll place one of those conch shells to our ears and listen. The sound of crashing waves and howling winds will take us back. To that day, we ran breathless along an empty Mexican beach. Hearts pumping…

Free!

The sun was breaking over Reynosa as we maneuvered through it, the Mexico of my youth upon me once more. Yet my thoughts were not on beaches or seashells, but on the road ahead. And figuring out how to traverse this magical country just as quickly as possible in order to return to the Pacific Ocean.

"*¡Aquí! ¡Aquí!*" Mari shouted, pointing to a rusty sign with faded numbers. I pulled the steering wheel hard to the right, barely making the turnoff. I looked in my side-view mirror and saw the trailer swaying wildly from one side of the road to the other. A moment of panic ensued as I envisioned the trailer somersaulting down the road, spilling out her guts along the way. A trail of books and junk left in her wake, scattered along the Mexican 101, as the Beast dragged the trailer along the asphalt. But the trailer succumbed, fell in line behind the truck, allowing me to relinquish those dreaded thoughts and plot our course. We'd head due south to the city of Tamaulipas, then onwards to Veracruz, where we'd take a much-needed rest.

A little over two hours into Mexico, as we made our way through Ciudad Victoria, a bright-white glove motioned for us to stop. My first reaction was to ignore it, pretend I hadn't seen it, but when I saw the man attached to the glove wearing a badge and a gun, I pumped the brakes. He was a short and portly fellow, with a thick, black mustache that stretched across his lip, then raced down and past the corners of his mouth. I half-expected him to be wearing a crisscross bandolier of bullets on his chest and chomping on a cigar.

"*Papeles,*" he said, staring hard and direct at our newly minted '*Transportista*' decal. I grabbed the plastic folder—kept at the ready—housing all of our travel papers and passports. I wasn't an idiot; I knew the drill. He scanned the thick pile of papers, then asked, rather tersely, "*¿A dónde vas?*"

"It's all right there in the papers," I said calmly, trying to maintain my cool.

"Where are you going?" he repeated, his agitation obviously growing.

My voice rose. "Nicaragua. Like I said, it's all right there in the papers." Mari grumbled something in Spanish. Some Nicaraguan slang that undoubtedly translated to, "Shut the fuck up, Kevin!"

The sheriff pushed back his wide-brimmed sombrero and brushed the sweat from his brow. Then he walked to the back of the truck. I was tempted to leave, to drive off and leave him in our dust. It didn't appear like he had any car or motorcycle with which to give chase. Perhaps he'd been dropped off there or walked from his home. But just as I was about to take off, I realized he still had our passports in his thick, leathery hands.

He returned to my window minutes later, talking excitedly in a thick accent and using a jumble of slang words and colloquialisms that I couldn't make out. It was as if each word he uttered was being filtered through a mouthful of syrup. Mari was as perplexed as me by this seemingly new language. My anxiety only rose as we sat on that dusty road listening to Pancho Villa, sheriff of Ciudad Victoria, rattle off indiscernible words like a machine gun spraying bullets.

"Despacio, despacio-Slowly, slowly," I pleaded, as the animated lawman turned a dark shade of red and talked even faster. I pointed to our passports that he held in his hand and pulled out the mythical manifest, holding it up in the air as a diversionary tactic, hoping to distract him from his ongoing diatribe. But Pancho Villa was wise, savvy to the gringo's ways, and continued on with his speech. Minutes later, came his last volley of gobbledygook—a last hurrah—before he stopped his incessant chatter and motioned for me to follow him. Oh great, I thought, this is where I die. Where Pancho Villa exacts retribution upon the white man for stealing his land and erecting a border across it. Where the scales of justice are realigned. Atonement delivered. Mari's eyes grew wide with alarm as I opened the door and exited the truck.

I followed the sheriff back, past the camper and trailer, my fate unknown. He ordered me to stop and face the trailer. My knees wobbled. I was about to punch my ticket. Check out. Right here on the side of the road in Ciudad Victoria. "¡*Mire!*" he said, spit spraying from his mouth. I looked around but saw nothing. Was he pointing to the spot where he'd soon stuff my dead, bullet-ridden body? Inside the trailer? If so, the joke would be on him. As he'd be tasked with unloading a thousand pounds of books before he could cram me inside.

"The lights…" he finally said in exasperation. "The lights!"

"The lights?" I repeated. "Which lights?"

"Those lights!" He pointed to the rear of the trailer.

"Which lights?" I was confused and wondering if I'd slipped into some sort of Mexican Abbott-and-Costello routine. He pointed to the corners of the trailer. "Hold on, are you talking about the brake lights?"

His eyes lit up as if he'd just discovered gold for the first time.

"No, no, no. Our brake lights work just fine. Here, let me show you." I felt the weight lifting off my shoulders. I was going to live. Pancho Villa didn't want to eradicate me from his land, after all. I practically skipped back to the truck, eager to prove our brake lights were in perfect operational order. I'd only made it halfway when he ordered me to return, sparking the old dread to come flooding back.

"Your lights are too narrow," said Pancho, pulling his sombrero down over his forehead and stopping just above his eyes.

"Too narrow?" I asked, drawing my words out in disdain. "Wait a minute," I paused and tried to regain my composure, before I completely lost my shit. "Now these lights work perfectly fine. Too narrow…that's not even a thing."

"Yes, they're too narrow," he repeated for the umpteenth time. "Somebody might not see them." He ratcheted his sombrero even farther down on his forehead until all I could see were two dark slits where his eyes used to be.

"With all due respect," I said, "half the cars down here don't even have brake lights. Or headlights, for that matter." I looked under the wide brim of his hat, searching for his eyes, but they seemed to have disappeared altogether. "Hell, some cars down here don't even have doors or windshields," I continued, my voice rising. "If this trailer can pass in the United States, it sure as shit can pass in Mexico!"

The sheriff, clearly displeased with my analysis of the Mexican vehicle, began spraying me, our general vicinity, and really the entire city of Ciudad Victoria with a blistering, profanity-laced tirade replete with every Spanish curse word known to man. Then, after completely wearing himself out, he pulled a wrinkled ticket book from his back pocket and told me I was either going to pay a fine or follow him back to the police station.

My first shakedown! I should have seen it coming. But I'd been in the states for too long, immune to the bribery and grift that comes as second nature in other countries. I'd have to readjust. To catch back on. But soon, it would be back, like acting in a play where you know all the lines, reprising an old role.

"Officer," I said, changing into character. "Can't we work this out some other way?"

Line cast…

"Well, the fine is rather steep," his voice trailed off, although I noted a marked improvement in his Spanish, absent of all the heavy slang. Even his eyes seemed to have reemerged from the witness protection program. "But maybe we can work something out."

Fish on!

A delicate dance of bribery ensued, one that went on far longer than need be. Perhaps due to my unfamiliar role as 'bribee' combined with a willingness to dance longer and fight harder—there was principal involved, after all—I presented my case with a vigor normally reserved for the Supreme Court, espousing the virtues of justice and righteousness to Pancho Villa, the irony completely lost on me. A nobility that would diminish with each succeeding town, as getting to our destination proved far 'loftier' than paying off the local cop.

But this first encounter was different. We were two gunslingers, squaring off on the edge of town. Staring into the other man's eyes, searching for his weakness, his vulnerability. There we stood, for a good half an hour, until Pancho Villa cracked.

"*¡Hijue puta!*" he screamed. "Just get the hell out of here! Hurry, hurry! Go! Go! Go!"

I sprinted back to the truck and sped away before he could change his mind. Mari looked at me with confusion. "*¿Que pasó?*" she asked.

"I don't know, he just let me go."

A surge of pride rippled through my belly as we motored along Carretera 101, having just escaped my first bribe. I paid little heed to the '*Transportista*' sticker spread across our windshield or the dark clouds rolling in from the south. Mari scooted across the bench and grabbed my hand. I felt her warmth and smiled.

***

"What are you doing here?" I asked.

Vek looked at me curiously, his blonde hair glowing under the moon. "Why is anyone anywhere?"

"Aw shit, not this again. What are you, fucking Socrates?"

He kept staring, undaunted by my reaction. "More importantly, why are *you* here?"

"Why am I here?" I echoed, readying myself for a verbal volley. But nothing came. Only silence.

"That's the question…"

"Why am I here?" I repeated, like a vinyl record with a gouge in it. "I'm here because…" I paused, searching for the words. The right words. Digging frantically through the shit-field of my mind. Beneath layers of trash and refuge, scraps of useless information and piles of discarded facts. I turned words over, seeking others below. New words. New ideas. Bits of wisdom. Shards of reasoning and purposeful conclusions. Yet I found none. I was digging through a parched desert. A barren wasteland. Wading through a scrapyard of crap in search of a pearl.

"I'm getting the fuck out of the rat race!" I finally screamed, sliding back into my old inner-city speak. Words be damned! Screw all that pesky, deep reasoning and self-reflective thought. Just spit out curse words when you draw a blank. Use them as adjectives and modifiers. Nouns and verbs. Make my Advanced English teachers proud.

"But why did you have to leave?" Vek asked. "What are you running from? Think, Kevin, think."

"Now, listen up, Plato. I'm not running *from* anything; I'm running *to* something."

There was that phrase again—the same one I'd given to the Peace Corps recruiter years before when she'd asked why I wanted to join. "I'm not running *from* anything," I had told her. "I'm running *to* something. The Peace Corps is calling me and has been for a long time." I'd meant every word, too. Something had been drawing me in, some external force beyond my understanding. Something intangible, yet powerful. Meaningful.

So, what was going on now? Why did I feel this unshakable desire to bail out on life and my flourishing new business career? Was I running *to* something this time, or was I just running? Running from conformity and responsibility. Running from booze and demons. Running from my past.

"Kevin, Kevin…" I opened my eyes and found Mari shaking me. "You're having a nightmare." I struggled to regain my bearings, to locate my spot in the world and the direction I was headed. I peeked out the camper window. The sun was rising, beaming her golden rays across the dirt lot we'd pulled into last night. A hen strutted across the lot, followed closely by a trail of chicks. A beautiful new day was upon us.

Mari scrambled up some eggs and beans, and then we got back on the road. We were in a flat, dusty part of Mexico, where the pace of life was slow and measured. We drove cautiously through one small ranch town after another, hoping to avoid the dreaded white glove, the hand of the man trying to flag us down. Toward midday, we found ourselves in a caravan of semi-trucks, flatbeds, and cars towing cars. All of us snaking our way through Mexico en route to Central America. Commercial vagabonds traveling along a modern-day silk road. From the deserts of northern Mexico to the tropics of Central

America. From sand to jungle. Gypsies we were. One and all. Wanderers. Seeking fortune and willing to risk life and limb to find it.

We moved farther into Mexico, lands where the great Aztec Empire once thrived. An empire stretching from the deep jungles in the south, teeming with wildlife and fauna, to the desert scrublands of the north. The lifeblood of humanity once pulsed here. Steady and strong. Its arteries twisting and turning, spreading into every person and spirit. Into every village and town. Until the Spaniards arrived, in search of gold and wealth, and ripped into those arteries with their lead and steel, drowning the land in blood.

The Beast rumbled through Cuauhtemoc, a gritty town named after the last ruler of the Aztec Empire. Cuauhtemoc rose to power upon the death of the great King Montezuma. Coronated during the siege of Tenochitlan (Mexico City), just as the Spanish were draining the final lifeforce from the land. But Cuauhtemoc did not waiver. He painted a black stripe down the center of his face, sprinkled it with iron pyrite, then grabbed his spear and his shield and set out to defend his people and their land. Cuauhtemoc wasn't running *from* anything. He was running *to* his destiny. His fate.

My fate—our fate—was less known, just a blank sheet of paper, with a sliver of moonlight illuminating its edges.

Chapter 19

Veracruz, a sleepy fishing town nestled on the shores of the Gulf of Mexico, was a kaleidoscope of color, from the turquoise waters and light-blue skies to the red pangas and purple houses. The snow-cone man added variety, drizzling cherry-red, lemon-yellow, and lime-green syrup over balls of ice. His sugary bottles glistened in the sun as he shaved blocks of ice across a blade dug into a slab of mahogany. Even the sun joined in on the fun, morphing from marmalade orange to Sangria red, sending barrages of color across the sky.

"I want that one," Mari said, pointing to the indigo-blue syrup. He drizzled the agave—thick as oil—over the shaved ice and handed it to her. "Mmmmm," Mari raved, smacking her sugary lips and licking her newly formed blue mustache. "Here, try some." She held the snow cone up to my mouth.

I took a bite and grinned. "Hey, why don't we stay here for a few days?" My sugar high allowed me to forget the long trek that still lay ahead as well as the cops who'd already pulled us over three times by then. Not to mention the fact that we were on the wrong coast of Mexico. But all that seemed trivial, now. Anecdotal. As I was more than content to live in this beautiful world of color.

Mari and I strolled along the boardwalk, arm in arm, watching children sprint across the sand as their parents sipped fruity drinks and peered out to the sea. Open-air cantinas and palm-frond huts lined the beach, their shelves filled with row upon row of rum. Endless bottles of sweet booze. We stopped at one hut and ordered Cóctel de Mariscos, a combination of fish, octopus, shrimp, diced onions, green pepper, cilantro, chili powder, and lime. A delicious blend of flavors, both bitter and spicy in equal measures.

But my eyes kept returning to the rum bottles, lined up in perfect rows, like obedient soldiers ready for battle. The clinking and clattering of bottles, the laughter, the scent of ripened pineapple and squishy mango sloshing around the rum—was like Pavlov's bell. I tried blocking out the smells and the noise as I bit into my chewy púlpo, my octopus. Mari smiled and took another bite, fish juice dripping down her chin, oblivious to the war being waged inside my head. I was a soldier, hunting down my prey, senses on high alert. Alcohol, my target. Alcohol, my enemy.

***

From that first drink year ago with the beautiful Carla Cameron, running through Regina's apartment without care, void of anxiety, bereft of that ever-present self-doubt—it was as if alcohol could lift the gloom. Strip away the unpleasantness within the world. Unfortunately, that faux freedom and quasi-happiness became etched into my brain, leaving an indelible mark. Alcohol fused with the desire for female companionship—a crossbreed of addictions that would trail me for years.

I bounced from female to female, never sticking around too long, always looking for the next. Next girl, next beer, next adventure. On the few occasions I did fall, I fell hard and fast, and was burned. Scars that were slow to heal. After high school, life became dull. Empty. Friends had fallen away, and I wasn't moving. I was stuck in neutral. Stuck in the mud. So, after piddling around junior college for a year, I made a move. I enrolled at Chico State, packed everything I owned into my Fiat X-19, and drove to Northern California. And once there, I was determined to make the most of it, cracking the books and putting in the work. But I was no fucking angel. And when the weekends game, I partied. Hard! This *was* Chico State, after all. Number one party school in the nation.

Now, going Greek—and I am referring to joining a fraternity here—was the last thing in the world I'd ever do, the whole 'conformity' and 'taking direction from others' being a bridge too far. Yet, still, I wanted to be a part of something. So, when a flier for Generating Developmental Ideas (GDI for short), a social club with an angle toward community service, circled the campus—I bit. I'd love to say that my interest was piqued by altruistic reasons—a budding desire to build strong community ties, and all. But, in truth, it was the weekly 'socials' (keggars) and one-to-one male to female membership that drew me in. I was a math guy and I liked the odds.

At our first meeting, held in one of Chico State's many lecture halls, the president, a short, muscular guy with jet-black hair, said that while our name was Generating Developmental Ideas or GDI to the outside world—internally, the letters GDI stood for God Damn Independence. Sign me the fuck up!

GDI wasn't so much anti-fraternity or sorority (although it was!) but more of a professional party club. With weekly theme parties and drinking events held at rented halls and event spaces, where we would dance, socialize, and drink. Emphasis on the drinking, as there would be multiple kegs at every party along with a shot station. Membership was limited to 100 men and 100 women, and cost $100 per semester, which included all the beers and shots you could drink. Like I said, I liked the math.

Our first party, the Social Roundup, was a western theme hoedown, held in an actual barn on the outskirts of town. Hay was scattered about the floor of the big, red building and Randy Travis was belting out twangy lyrics from a set of giant speakers tied to the rafters. I made my way to the keg, still wearing my customary board shorts and T-shirt—exercising my own 'God Damn Independence.' I didn't really 'do' country. In fact, I was disappointed that our first party and my introduction to GDI had anything to do with Clint Black, George Strait or Reba McEntire whatsoever. But after a few cold ones, mixed in with a couple kamikazes, and watching pretty girls in tight jeans and cowboy hats strut by—I reconsidered my opposition to Country.

It was her hair that I noticed first, long and blonde and cascading down her back, below the white cowboy hat she wore tilted to one side. But when she walked by, it was her swagger that really got me. A sexy-as-all-hell strut. Her boots, reaching up to her knees, oozing confidence with every step. I angled toward her; the alcohol pushing me forward, summoning my own cowboy swagger. She halted and turned back, looking me straight in the eyes. I froze, barely able to breathe, a million words flooding my brain. But when none came, my feet took control, pushing my body forward. Walking right past her as if she didn't even exist. As if she were just another obstacle between me and the keg. That precious, beautiful keg. In other words, I choked. Pussed out!

I spent the rest of the night drinking and flirting with other girls, while keeping my head on a swivel, searching for the girl with the boots and the strut. At some point, I gave up, assuming she'd left the party. But later that evening, after I was nice and lubed, she appeared once again. Only this time, walking right past me as if I didn't exist.

She stopped at the kamikaze bar and raised her hand for a drink. I grabbed a piece of straw off the ground, stuck it in my teeth, and then moseyed up to the bar. "Howdie, ma'am," I said, rolling the straw between my teeth. I was cocky as a motherfucker by then, what with all the booze sloshing around inside my belly. She gave a playful smile, her light brown eyes emitting equal measures of curiosity and indifference.

"Did I miss something?" she asked, looking down at my sandals and trunks. "Is there a beach nearby?"

"Right outside. Wanna go for a dip?"

"Hmmm, let me guess," she said, plucking the straw from my teeth. "Clothing optional?"

"Well, of course, darling," I said in my best country drawl.

"I'll pass." Her eyes were soft, questioning.

"Let me guess…you're from Texas. Studying…psychology!"

"Wow, you're just full of confidence, aren't you?"

"Why, yes, ma'am. I'm just an old country boy at heart."

"Yeah, I could tell by the flip-flops. By the way, Communications, not Psychology. And San Antonio, Texas, to be precise. Now, it's my turn. Southern California, obviously. Perhaps…Los Angeles, or maybe San Diego? And Business, of course…because you just couldn't quite cut it in engineering."

A grin spread across my face. "Nice! So…your place or mine?"

She stared a moment longer, then flicked the straw and walked away. "Hey, I'm Kevin…by the way…just in case you were wondering."

Then I was alone. Alone with my beers, and my kamikazes, and my over-inflated, booze-soaked ego. Gravity appeared, tilting me forty degrees to the south. The music faded, siphoned into a black hole. I shifted my weight forty degrees to the north and headed out of the barn.

A warm summer's eve greeted me, sticky and pungent. I put my head down and began the long walk back to my apartment, moving quickly past newly formed couples with tongues down each other's throats, and circles of friends making their last farewells. I scanned the ground, searching for any obstacles that might trip me up: blades of grass, dirt…smooth cement.

"Bye, Kevin…" The words rained down from above. I stopped and peered into the sky, gazing past black holes and dimming stars, searching for a message within clouds of apathy and blurred vision.

"Goodbye, Kevin!" The words traveled along conventional sound waves this time, allowing me to triangulate and pinpoint its origin. The signal was coming from the girl with the light-brown eyes and cowboy hat that rode askew of her long, blonde hair. The girl with the strut. "Ma'am," I said, fake tipping my imaginary cowboy hat. I heard some giggles from her group of friends as they walked toward the dorms.

She smiled, "I'm Jen, by the way…just in case you were wondering," then disappeared into the night. Evaporated into the ether. Perhaps the universe. While I stumbled through the streets of Chico in search of my bed. Heart racing. Apathy dissolving.

***

By our second day in Veracruz, Mari and I had settled into a nice little rhythm—decompressing and learning to embrace our new roles of wanderers of Earth. Our old lives—and the accompanying stress it once contained—were fading from our memory banks just as quickly as our new reality was setting in.

We strolled along Veracruz's cobblestone streets, poking our heads into trinket shops, candy stores, and coffeehouses. We stopped at the beautiful *Catedral Veracruz*, a seventeenth-century church, boasting a three-stage tower on its right, and a massive, octagonal dome in the center.

Its ornate and centuries-old wooden doors—silent and serene in their grand archway—beckoned us inside. As we entered the cathedral, our eyes were immediately drawn to the alabaster columns and mahogany crossbeams that seemed to rise into the heavens. We paused and took in the reverent scene. Embracing the spiritual calm. On the far wall was a giant cross. Jesus was upon it. Peering down. Blood dripped from his forehead, embedded with a crown of thorns. *Sacrifice.* The word rattled around inside my brain. What does it mean to sacrifice? To *truly* sacrifice?

Mari ushered me into a row of pews. The wood, old and chunky, wrinkled and gnarled—engrained with burls and swirls. Each ring revealing a chapter in the long and storied life of this majestic tree. Dwelling here, now. Quietly and solemnly serving the church, welcoming visitors from around the world. "Sit here, my friend, and your troubles will fade away," it whispers. "Allow my life force to flow into you, and your pain will be no more." And here this majestic old tree will sit. For all eternity. Having given up its life for others…*Sacrifice.*

A family hurried to the front of the church, stopping at the base of Jesus, just below his feet and downcast eyes. They looked up as one and made the sign of the cross, then sank to their knees and bowed their heads. The mother caressed a string of rosary beads while humming a prayer. The father tapped his daughter's shoulder and motioned for her to bow her head lower. Their devotion struck a chord. I'd seen it once before. Felt it once before. Years ago, but the memory stuck…

Melvin Michael Cromley, my father, strode through St. Therese's Catholic Parish with purpose, his four kids—me included—tagging close behind, our eyes wide with wonder at the strange, new sights: the massive crowd of people, all decked out in their Sunday best; the weird-smelling smoke rising from golden lanterns; and the biblical figures etched in glass, so lifelike they appeared to be leaping off the walls, into present day, their eyes following us as we moved through the church.

I stayed close to my father's hip, studying his every move as we traversed this peculiar landscape, he'd brought us to in the middle of the night on Christmas Eve. He stopped suddenly and moved down one aisle. We followed close behind and took a seat on the bench. That's when I saw it, saw him make that gesture. That submission. Saw him drop to his knees and sink his chin down to his chest. I turned and studied my sisters' faces, waiting for their reaction. Searching for an answer, some reasoning to make sense of my father's actions, always so strong and confident, like a superhero in the movies. But now here he was on his knees, head lowered, making some sort of hand motion across his chest. What did it all mean—these strange things I was witnessing?

My sisters quickly followed, falling to their knees, one after the other, then planting their chins upon their chests. I looked around the church, alarmed and somewhat confused by all the people on their knees. My eyes rose to the images on the walls. Scenes so brilliant and colorful—so vivid—I felt my body falling, transported to the banks of the Red Sea. I stood with a band of soldiers, clutching our spears and our shields as we prepared for battle. Suddenly, it was nighttime, a million stars overhead, as I kneeled in a patch of hay staring at a newborn baby. Then the skies turned black, and the baby disappeared. I was no longer kneeling but standing at the foot of a cross. A man was stretched out along its trunk, iron spikes plunged deep into his wrists.

I felt my body falling again, plunging down. Farther and farther, I fell, my breathing labored. I opened my eyes. My father was tugging on my shirt, sliding me off the bench. Moments later, I was on the floor, straightening my special dress shirt, the one with the stiff collar that pinched my neck. Then, I let my chin fall obsequiously to my chest, just as my father had.

My eyes wanted to return to the images on the wall, to frolic amidst the fields and rivers. But I kept my head down, staring at the wooden floor, mentally tracing the swirls and curves as if moving through a miniature maze. In time, my eyes grew weary. I let them shut, embracing the stillness. A sudden rush of sadness came over me. I breathed in slowly, allowing the air to penetrate deep into my lungs. Exhaling, I felt a release, like catching my breath after a long run. A lump formed in my throat, followed by that miserable pain that lodges inside my nose whenever I fight back my tears.

But I couldn't hold them back, not this time, no matter how hard I tried. They escaped through the corners of my clenched eyelids. Two sad and lonely tears streaking down my cheeks, tears I'd suppressed for far too long. But my strength was waning, my body failing. Failing to hide its feelings, failing to mask its pain. I opened my eyes and gazed at the cross on the far side of the wall, peering at the man upon it through blurry, red eyes. Such pain he must have felt that day. Suffered that day. I closed my eyes and whispered, "I'm sorry, God," in my softest voice.

Chapter 20

The Beast motored on, through rolling hills and small towns, as Veracruz became just a distant memory. A footnote in our fledgling saga. Mountain peaks appeared in the distance, dark-green and lush, like camouflaged soldiers peeking up through the clouds. A calmness pervaded the land, eroding the chaotic energy I'd always known. Reducing the distance between me and the land. The Earth. Between me and life itself.

We arrived at the foot of the mountains, passing through a quiet pueblo whose residents appeared to be sleeping off their tequila nightcaps. Upon our exit, a menacing white glove flagged us down. The owner of the glove belonged to a baby-faced cop with a wispy mustache—just a line, really—and wide, buggy eyes. He could barely contain his excitement while asking for our *'papeles,'* his voice breathy and full of zeal.

And so, the routine began, each of us playing our parts as we have so many times before. The back-and-forth, the push-and-pull, the tug-of-war. Until the offer is finally made, "*Señor*, maybe you'd like to just pay your fine here…"

This is where I feign ignorance. "Fine, what fine?" As if I'm unaware of the little game we're currently playing, and ignorant of its rules.

But I do know the game. In fact, I know it very well. First, they find some random, bogus infraction, while shaking their head and pretending to be sympathetic to my plight. You see, they don't really want to trouble me, but the violation—the Code—mandates that they act. Then comes the whole cat-and-mouse charade, which lasts five to ten minutes, with the cop digging around in his codebook, searching for some arbitrary infraction that doesn't even apply to me. Finally, I'm given the option of following him back to the station where I can pay the fine and have my driver's license returned.

But what I've learned over time is, the longer I can keep him arguing on the side of the road, the lower my fine becomes. What I'm really hoping for is that he becomes so tired of playing our little game, of arguing with the confused gringo, that he blurts out the five-word sentence known to every cop in Mexico. A sentence I can only assume they're taught on the first day of the Academy, "*Deme algo por las aguas*," which translates roughly to: "Well, at least buy me water." Or in gringo terms, "Give me a couple bucks or I'm going to keep fucking with you."

After arriving at this point in our little theater of the absurd—well past the big-dollar bribes—I'm free to offer him whatever I want. Within reason, of course, we wouldn't want to offend his sense of dignity by handing him a pile of nickels and dimes. A dollar or two will normally do the trick, sending me on my merry way.

But this time was different. My patience had run its course. The whole bullshit pretense was boiling my blood, turning my neck a crimson red, pressing a red-hot iron against my back. Macabre thoughts raced through my mind, of me reaching through the window and grabbing the young cop by his neck, choking him out right there on that steamy, crumbling highway. This boy cop, no older than me, 29, shaking me down in the middle of fucking nowhere.

My muscles and tendons constricted, my hand wrenching itself into a claw. I was a cobra ready to strike, sweating and seething in our F250 truck. Our camper and current home lowered into its back, the corrugated-metal walls stained brown from Texas sand and Mexican dirt. Our trailer, tagging close behind, filled with a life's worth of 'things.' Worldly possessions. Yes, the ol' trailer of shit, crammed with books and ripped-up jeans, ratty t-shirts and old journals. Love letters from past flames and wrestling trophies from bygone days. All of it, the entirety of one's life, sandwiched between six planks of wood, a 4×6' rectangular box riding atop a trailer.

That's where I found myself, arguing with a dirty cop with a sissy voice and a wannabe mustache. But what do you do? *What in the fuck do you do?* Mari touched my leg, which had transformed into a block of cinder, along with the rest of my body. I turned and faced her, a kettle nearing its boil. Her eyes had always soothed me, calmed me, speaking a million words with a single glance. But today those eyes were different. Serious. Stating absolutely and unequivocally, "Just shut the hell up and pay this little bastard, so we can continue our journey into those beautiful Oaxacan Mountains."

I complied, holding out two crisp, one-dollar bills with my claw. The young cop took my money with his white glove, then motioned for me to proceed. I put the Beast in gear, smiled, and said, "Gracias."

That sense of freedom we'd tasted in Veracruz, like a tulip in full bloom, reemerged as we climbed the mountains of Oaxaca, prickly seeds of life that open your heart and thaw your soul. The oxygen, seeping out from the wrinkled bark of trees, cooled and refined by the rich, black soil—the Earth's lungs—made for mountain air so crisp and pure, it cleansed your mind. We inhaled deeply, drinking it in. Our first pure breaths in years. Mari smiled, sensing she was amidst her ancestral land.

Oaxaca stretched into Chiapas, where the trees grew taller and the mountains higher. Mayans once wandered this land, breathed this rich air, beginning about 3,400 years ago and lasting nearly 2,000 years, building magnificent cities and pyramids, and creating one of the most advanced civilizations known to man. Mari's bloodline ran through these mountains, coursing all the way to Nicaragua.

The Zapatista Army now hid among these trees, having recently declared war on the Mexican government, fighting for the rights of peasants and the indigenous people. These mountains, and the shadows they cast, held mysteries that ran deep. Mysteries buried in the dirt, rooted in the soil, forever scratching at the surface above.

"What's that smell?" Mari asked, scrunching her nose as we rounded a bend. She had a keen sense of smell, always plucking the leaves off of trees and plants, holding them to her nose and breathing in their knowledge.

"What smell?"

"It smells like *hule*—rubber," she said, glancing out her side-view mirror.

I checked my side-view mirror but saw nothing of note. Just then a stinky smell hit my nose, reminiscent of that stench you get when you forget to take your parking brake off and drive for a few blocks. Something was definitely burning. *Shit, please don't let it be the engine!* My neck tightened as I peered toward the hood. No smoke. *Yes!* After looking slowly from one side-view mirror to the other, I finally spotted it, a small trail of smoke coming from the rear, perhaps from the trailer. But there was nothing mechanical back there, no transmission or engine. Perhaps we'd blown a tire. I found an empty spot on the side of the road and eased the Beast over.

We hurried to the back of the trailer, where we got a full dose of the acrid smoke. I poked around, looking for a flat tire, but didn't find any. "*¡Aquí!*"

Mari hollered. Jogging around the trailer, I saw her pointing to a stream of black smoke rising up from the wheel well. Moving in for a closer look, I discovered the trailer was riding just a few millimeters above the tire. I crawled under the chassis and looked. The bracket attaching the wheel well to the trailer's frame had buckled, presumably under all the weight we'd tasked it to support. Now, every time we banged into a pothole or ricocheted over a dip, the tire scraped against steel, leaving pits and gouges in the rubber. It was only a matter of time before it ruptured altogether.

"We can't drive this fucking thing, not like that!" My voice echoed across a forest of trees, our interlude of calmness coming to a screeching halt. Mari rushed inside the camper, returning with my toolbox and an eager expression on her face. "No, Mari, I can't fix this. Look at the metal bar right there…see how it's all bent? A ratchet ain't gonna fix that."

Just up the road, under a massive Ceiba tree, stood a huge tractor tire buried halfway up in the dirt, with the words 'Se Vulcaniza' painted in white lettering along its sidewalls. I knew from living in Nicaragua that these silent road markers, like angels of the highway, meant a tire shop was nearby.

We found a slender, gray-haired man prying the tire off an old, beater rim, just off the highway. "*Buenas,*" I called out. Startled, he dropped his crowbar and jumped to his feet.

"*Buenas,*" he replied, wiping sweat and grease off his brow. After a brief rundown of our current predicament, he readily agreed to follow us back to the truck.

After sliding under the trailer and crawling around for a bit, he emerged. "You need some fresh welds and a new tire…" he began, pulling a dirty rag from his back pocket and wiping his hands. "Now, I can weld those brackets, but I don't have that type of tire. It's unusually small. We don't see many of those around here."

I'd paid little attention to the trailer tires before, but now that he mentioned it, they were rather small. Perhaps I should have noticed that before loading all my precious books and cargo atop the tiny clown tires and feeble suspension. Twenty minutes later, he was back with a welder, a jack, and two young helpers I assumed were his sons. They attempted to jack up the trailer but failed, so I jumped in, providing an extra set of hands and a tad more brawn. "*¿Que hay dentro*—What's inside?" asked the old man, as the four of us cranked on the jack, straining with all our might. He probably thought I had dead bodies stacked up inside our little wood coffin.

"Tools," I replied, face smashed against the splintery box, using my legs as leverage to lift the godawful trailer. Knowing full well that 'tools' was the farthest thing from the truth. And that a cargo of dead bodies would have been preferable—less embarrassing—than the cold, hard truth: I had a trailer full of shit! And books…lots and lots of books.

"Pues, es demasiado pesado—Well, it's too heavy," he finally said.

We released our grips and watched the trailer sink back into the road. Then, for the next half hour, Mari and I pulled boxes from the cramped trailer, stacking them in neat rows alongside the freeway, as 18-wheelers blew by, tooting their horns and kicking up dust. When the old man determined the trailer was light enough, we set about cranking it up once more. This time meeting with success.

They pried off the tire in record time, then slipped under the chassis and welded. Sparks flew out from either side of the coffin as he welded chunks of metal to the undercarriage where the struts had collapsed. The welds and brackets were soon melded together, appearing stronger and more reliable than the original design. I asked him to beef up the other side as well, prompting his sons to sprint back to the house for additional metal rods and cinder blocks to rest the trailer on. He continued welding, adding additional plates and rods until the undercarriage looked like a fortified tank.

When he finished welding, he told us he could patch the tire back at his shop. We agreed. Not wanting to overload the trailer again, we shoved the bulk of the boxes inside the camper and then followed him back to his house, which was equal parts home, garage, and outdoor workshop. He offered us Tamarindo, a tangy juice made from the meaty fruit which grows inside pods on the Tamarind tree. Then he set about burning chunks of rubber onto our miniature clown tire, melting the material into the pits and gouges. It was only a patch, he said, to hold us over until we could find a replacement. His sons appeared holding glasses of the brownish juice. It was cool and refreshing, like a slice of heaven, as we sat there in wooden rocking chairs sweating, the heat gathering strength, approaching 100 degrees. Add to it the humidity, and we soon felt like we were in a sauna, with water dripping on the hot coals.

He cut additional scraps of rubber off an old tire, formed them into thin strips and glued them onto the tire. After burning the rubber on with a torch, he dipped the entire Frankenstein monstrosity into a barrel of dirty water. A hiss rang out when the hot rubber touched the water, followed by a poof of steam which rose into the thick sky.

I couldn't help but notice his demeanor, so calm and cool, so matter of fact, as he went about his business, shuttling from one workstation to the next, between the workbench and the torch area, the compressor, and the tire barrel—always humming and smiling. Such a far cry from the raving lunatic I became at the first sign of trouble. He'd worked for two hours straight and not bitched once, while I'd cursed every swear word known to man in the brief few minutes it took me to assess the problem. *Just relax and take life slow,* his actions seemed to say, as he slid the disfigured clown tire onto the trailer's axle and cranked the lug nuts tight. I tried to inhale his presence, to breathe in a sliver of his Zen.

"Cien pesos."

After some quick mental math, I realized he wanted less than $10 for all that work. Ten freaking dollars to save my ass, to get us back on the road, to impart a measure of serenity upon my soul. I handed him a twenty and told him to keep the difference, then passed out a couple of bucks to the boys.

We honked and shouted, "¡Gracias! ¡Gracias!" as we drove away, passing the giant 'Se Vulcaniza' tire as we pulled onto the highway. The translation of which, I decided, means: "Here resides a saint for all ye weary and broken travelers." The Beast let out a roar and hurtled down the road.

Always forward.

Chapter 21

The Mayans didn't believe in time like you and I. Where events such as births, deaths, and marriage are plotted in an orderly fashion along a linear calendar, like pinpricks along a path. No, the Mayans marked life and time in a circular pattern, like celestial moons orbiting a planet. The Universe was a giant wheel, slowly spinning, important events repeating.

I thought about time as continuity, and repeating events, while trudging to the back of the trailer. It had only been a few hours since the old man had welded the undercarriage, yet we were hearing banging and thudding coming from the same location. The noise became so loud, I thought we might be dragging a dead antelope through the Chiapas Mountains. As I neared the trailer, a drop of water fell on my head. Looking up, I spotted a patch of black ink in the sky, a pillow of darkness within a sea of blue. Was this lonely black cloud a message? A friendly reminder that Mother Nature was a guest on our trip. To further cement the message, as I kneeled down and prepared to crawl under the trailer for the umpteenth time, the patch of ink opened up, dumping an Olympic-sized pool of water on top of me. I twisted sideways and scooted under the coffin, as rain splattered against my cheek.

I located the recent weld job and metal plates, all of which appeared to be fine. Nothing broken as far as I could tell. I craned my neck and surveyed the wheel well on the far side. Everything looked good there, too. Unable to locate a dying carcass spinning around the axle, I laid my head down in the mud and stared up at the fire-engine-red frame, pondering our situation, as rain poured down, forming puddles all around me. I sank into the Earth, becoming one with the land. Yet, for some odd reason, I didn't get mad. Didn't scream or cuss. In fact, I was anything but mad. The rain and the mud, the problems, the setbacks—all seemed to fade away. A sense of peace filled the void, working its way up my spine and into my brain, then out to the tips of my fingers and my toes. I smiled, realizing I was in a moment of Zen. The old man's essence really *had* rubbed off on me. And the Universe, now dancing before me, was acting out its part. There were no linear calendars here. No carefully plotted pinpricks. Just life, burning bright, hurtling us through space. And I was along for the ride—this magical, glorious ride. Here. In Oaxaca. Under this trailer. This godforsaken trailer, crammed with every kind of worthless shit, all of it sitting just inches away from my face.

Water seeped through my shoes and chilled my toes, thrusting me back to Earth. I scooted out from the trailer and back into the rain. Readying myself to stand, I spotted the flat trailer tire. I wondered how I'd missed it. Searching for something complex when the solution was so simple. Perhaps our minds are predisposed to search for the complex, to weed through chaos and plumb confusion. But what if we could shut off that filter, allow our minds to wade through shallow waters? To focus on the underbelly of life—the struts and chassis that comprise all things. Maybe then, during that momentary lull, that respite from chaos, we become privy to the symphony of life. The harmony of nature. That special place where Zen lives.

"*¿Que es?*" Mari asked, as I jumped inside the truck. She looked me up and down, her eyes registering alarm as buckets of water drained off me. I looked like a rabid animal, my fur soaked to the bone. I could read her face. She was waiting for the storm, wondering why I wasn't screaming or pounding my fists on the steering wheel.

"Flat tire," I said with a chuckle. "Just a flat." My chuckle turned into a laugh, a low baritone chortle rising from my bowels. Mari's eyes widened as she stared at the wild beast that had replaced her husband. "It's just a flat," I repeated, through bursts of laughter. Her face eventually softened, recognizing the madman she'd married, as I continued to shout, "It's just a flat tire! It's just a flat tire!"

***

The next time I saw Jen was at our weekly GDI meeting, standing on the stairs and chatting with a group of friends, while I laid low in a corner of the lecture hall, stealing glances, and pretending not to notice her. Turning my head every time she glance my way. Jen, who?

The club's President began the meeting, providing details on the upcoming party. The 'get-to-know-you' social would take place in a rented hall on Nord

Avenue, the main drag of Chico. He discussed some upcoming volunteer work, preparations for Rancho Chico Days, a citywide festival that was planned for the following semester. Formerly known as Pioneer Days, they had canceled it a few years back because of the wild and drunken antics of a few thousand college kids, as well as the full-on riot that raged across the city for two days. Chico State's President Wilson having announced at the time that he'd 'taken Pioneer Days out back and shot it in the head.' But with a revamped name, and emphasis on community development, the parade, music and festival were back on. What could possibly go wrong?

When the meeting concluded, I purposely walked down Jen's side of the hall. She had her back to me as I made my way down the stairs, so I kept moving, figuring she couldn't see me. But then I felt a tug on the back of my shirt, a magical tug, and my heart raced. I turned around, smug, trying to hide my smile. But it wasn't Jen that had pulled my shirt. It was my roommate, Kenny. "Hey, we're going up to the Bear for some beers."

The Bear was a bar right next to campus, infamous for drunken tricycle races, a multitude of Sierra Nevada beers on tap, and its two stories of debauchery that played out every weekend. More importantly, it was where all our fake IDs worked like clockwork. Looking around for Jen, I realized she'd already passed me and was heading out the door. No look back, no meeting of the eyes. Nothing. The high I'd felt just milliseconds before came crashing to the ground.

"Okay," I told Kenny, and continued down the stairs. How is it you can tiptoe on top of the world in one moment and then plunge into the sea the next? But that would all be irrelevant, soon, as I polluted my body with copious amounts of Sierra Nevada, oblivious to the trials and tribulations of life and the female species.

Walking outside, we were met with a gush of warm air. I breathed in the dusk, mission set, Jen fading from my mind. Yet fate was lurking near, sharpening her quiver as she hid in the bough of a maple tree, its leaves glowing red in the fading sun. That's where I spotted Jen, under those very limbs, laughing and breathing in its bouquet with that same clique of friends. Rich girls, no doubt. Although everybody seemed rich when compared to me.

"Hey, there, cowboy," she said, as I walked by, trying to stop my knees from buckling.

I twirled an imaginary lasso above my head and tossed it her way, pretending to rein her in. She smiled. "It's not that easy." Her confidence was sexy as hell. There was no denying it. I wanted her something fierce.

I felt the ice rushing inside of my veins. "Wait a minute…do I know you?"

Her eyes sparkled like the glitter on a child's coloring book. A moment of wonder, of doubt. The blacks of her irises sharpening, focusing, training their sights on me. Then came a flutter, a dilation, and that sexy-as-all-hell confidence came roaring back. "No, I don't think you do…" She turned and continued chatting with her friends, ignoring me as if I was just another maple tree shedding its leaves. A momentary distraction. Now I was having a moment of wonder, of doubt.

"Bye…" I said, my voice echoing across the trees, spreading from limb to limb and branch to branch, fading at the tips of the gold and red leaves.

By the tender age of 19, I'd already built up a hefty cargo of cynicism toward my fellow man—or woman, as was the case. They all acted the same, in predictable ways, like controlled subjects in a lab. Obsequiously following, reacting in predictable ways to a stated hypothesis, beguiled by stimuli. Never deviating from the norm. But Jen seemed different, less predictable, making me want to shatter my beakers and burn my lab coat. Jen was unique.

***

"Pass me the socket wrench," the *Se Vulcaniza* mechanic said to his daughter, who couldn't have been over ten years old at most. I'd dragged the trailer and its flat tire three miles down the road, in pouring rain, to the nearest roadside angel. After telling us the wheel wells still weren't sturdy enough to withstand all the weight riding on it, Mari and I pulled out more boxes from her belly and stuffed them into the camper, leaving little room to maneuver through the kitchen or sitting area, as every square inch was now chockful of boxes and plastic bins.

Sparks spilled out from under the trailer as the mechanic welded even more metal struts and brackets across the frame. He repatched the tire, which had worn down, and suggested we fill it with a polymer substance that would solidify them. Since it meant no more flat tires, we agreed and told him to fill them both. Two hours later, we were back on the road, driving at a steady clip toward the Pacific Ocean. The trailer shaking and rattling like some rickety old carnival ride each time one of its rock-hard tires hit a pothole.

I wondered how in the world the tires would ever make it, traversing these shitty, crater-infested roads with 2,000 miles left to go. The pressure was taking its toll. My shoulders ached nonstop, and I'd begun driving hunched over like Igor. When we finally pulled over for lunch at a little taco stand on the side of the road, I told Mari that I no longer wanted to camp out and surf in Puerto Escondido and Puerto Angel. Something was out of whack. A stench in the air, foul and disconcerting. My moment of Zen had faded and the last thing on my mind was surfing and camping. I just wanted to make a beeline for Nicaragua, get there as soon as possible, and begin our new life. Mari readily agreed, eager to see her family and friends whom she hadn't seen in years. And not at all interested in surfing or fishing to begin with.

Emerging from the mountains and trees, we followed the road to my beloved Pacific Ocean. She appeared so serene, welcoming us home. Puerto Escondido, with its beautiful surf, lay just up the road. But we veered south and followed the coast to the city of La Ventosa, where we were immediately flagged down. La Ventosa (meaning *The Windy*) had been aptly named. As the wind blew so hard, I could barely open the truck door. Wind gusts of fifty knots.

The moment I exited the Beast, the door slammed shut behind me. I leaned forward and pushed my way through the wind, reaching the rear of the vehicle where a cop waited to begin 'negotiations.' Looking back, I noticed our rig was leaning heavily to one side. The cop began his usual routine, listing all my supposed infractions, as wind slashed our faces. We bent forward, practically curling into balls, to avoid being blown away. He clung desperately to his hat, ignoring the gun and jacket violently whipping about.

We skipped the usual perfunctory script and got down to brass tacks. I looked again at the truck and camper, noting the precarious angle it skewed, as wind barreled into its side. Just past the cop, to the south, the skies were turning an ominous black. As if the devil's army was flooding out of hell and marching toward La Ventosa. The cop followed my eyes. "*Viene una tormenta*—A storm is coming," he said in a low voice, as I handed him three dollars and walked away.

"*¡Oye!*" he shouted through the howling wind. "You should stop and wait for the storm to pass." I fought my way back to the truck, hopped inside, and cranked up the engine. The last thing I needed was advice from some corrupt cop. I was getting to Nicaragua, one way or another. Devil's army? Fuck them! Just try to stop me.

Chapter 22

Pre-party, it's called, getting nice and lubed before hitting the parties. The advantages are obvious: saving money, since you won't need to buy as many drinks wherever you end up that evening; Avoiding the sad desperation inherent in every keg line, as you creep ever so slowly to your steel god; and, swagger, that all-important element needed when conversing with the fairer sex.

Fortunately, my roommates and I could set aside these perfunctory motions of slamming cheap beer and drinking copious shots of Jägermeister, as our membership into GDI allowed for all the booze we could consume at the low, low price of $100 per semester. Beers and shots to our heart's content. Well…on the nights when they threw parties, anyway. It was the deal of the century. They even provided 'chaperones,' a handful of members who remained sober during the wild bacchanals, comforting the wobblers and vomiters, and giving rides to the idiots who drove.

The 'get-to-know-you' social was in full effect when we arrived inside a long, expansive hall, with kegs strategically placed in every corner and a kamikaze station near the back. Hundreds of metal folding chairs formed a giant circle around the edges of the room, with an equal number of red balloons sitting in the middle. I wondered what kind of drunken shenanigans this would entail, as my roommates and I headed for a keg. With our cups overflowing with prized Sierra Nevada ale, we moved onto the shot station for a kamikaze—or three.

I looked for Jen among the balloons and beer lines and people dancing. The hall was crowded and loud. After several more trips to the keg and shot station, a warm and fuzzy feeling took hold, like crawling into a cocoon. A garbled voice came over the PA, telling the men to find a chair within the circle and take a seat. The women were then directed to stand in front of a man. It all made sense now, the club's equal distribution of 100 men to 100 women—such wisdom.

"Now, sit on your partner's lap and *get-to-know-him*," said the PA voice, followed by an earsplitting whistle. I flinched, creating a tidal wave of beer, which splashed over the rim, down my arm, and onto my thighs, just as a plump and overly cheery brunette plopped down on my lap.

"Hi, there, I'm Samantha. What's your name? Where are you from? Why did you join GDI? Where do you live?" she belted out, oblivious to the beer she was sopping up with her sizable derriere. I tried uttering a response through her verbal melee, while wiping beer off my arm and the back of my hand, periodically shifting my butt to offset some of her weight. I'd barely said three words when the whistle rang out, sending the fair maiden down the line.

A petite blonde quickly replaced her, giving my skinny legs a much-needed rest. She scooted in closer, laughing about the silly game, the wind catching my sails. But then, like ticking gears, the whistle blew. Sixty seconds had elapsed. I held her hand as she drifted away. A busty, redhead took her spot, telling jokes for the entire minute. "What color are my eyes?" she asked, shutting them tight.

"Umm…green?" I probed, averting my eyes from her voluptuous tank top.

"No," she said, as the whistle blew, "they're double Ds."

And so, the night progressed, a bevy of women spinning in and out of my life in quick secession, interrupted only by the occasional bathroom break, beer refill, or that all-important kamikaze shot. Periodically, during one of these 60-second spurts of romance, we were given dares to complete: kiss your partner on the cheek; tell them something secret about yourself that nobody else knows; pick out their best feature and describe why you like it. Heated debates soon arose over whether one's boobs were better than their ass, as alcohol and the proximity to the opposite sex fueled a tense, sexually charged atmosphere.

Over time, the rapid influx of women became too much. I felt like an aging rock star on his farewell tour. The voice returned over the PA, telling the men to stand and for the women to sit. I stood, letting a cute girl with curls take my chair, hovering above her like a vulture circling his prey, not liking the new arrangement so much. When the whistle blew, I sat down, trying to distribute my weight equally across her legs, even though I only weighed about a buck forty soaking wet. It was my turn to say something witty, to make my case in sixty-seconds flat, before they rotated me out like an old pair of shoes. "Fancy meeting you here," I quipped, initially anyway, before moving on to the somewhat wittier 'Anybody sitting here?' as my skinny ass burrowed into their thighs. My buzz reaching new heights, I wrapped my arm tight around their shoulders, hoping to avoid falling unceremoniously to the floor.

During my circuit around the room, I began seeing two girls per lap. My once witty and semi-cerebral pickup lines devolving into something more rudimentary and crasser: "Let me ease that sexual tension you're feeling," and "Let's talk about the first thing that pops up," or the professorial, "Take me home, baby!"

"Oh, no, it's *you*," I heard, while sliding onto my next lap and readying a zinger. My pupils dialed in like shutters on a camera, into focus came Jen, clear and unobstructed. My witty repartee crumbled, disintegrated into a pile of rubble, as I sat there on her lap, like a little boy, staring into her eyes. Talk about losing your masculinity.

"Have you been good?" she chided, the power roles kicking full throttle into reverse. My brain, fading into a fog, scrambled for some measure of intellect. A nugget to toss her way, worthy of her mental acuity.

"Never," is what I came up with, slipping my arm around her shoulder and steadying myself for the ride. My eyes fell straight to her cleavage, that magical crease that drives a man mad, and her boobs jutting out like the pyramids of Giza. An electric pulse raced through my body, zipping from my brain to my groin in a matter of milliseconds. I felt myself getting hard. *Stop, Kevin.* I shifted my eyes from her chest to her long blonde hair, then over to her eyes— hoping to coax myself down from the erection cliff where I now stood. *Focus, Kev, focus.*

The party guide's voice rang out over the speakers, directing the men to grab a balloon from the pile in the center and to return to our partners. My face tuned bright red, knowing my boner would be on full display. "You, ok?" Jen asked, as I stood and did some quick, Houdini-style contortion inside my boxers and preyed the low lighting and drunkenness of my fellow revelers would be enough to obscure it. Turns out, I had nothing to worry about, as everybody was just as wobbly as me, paying my spry, new friend little heed as I walked to the center of the room and grabbed a balloon.

"Of all my luck," Jen joked, as they explained the rules of the game. I placed the balloon between our chests, my fingers brushing against her breasts. "Yes, it must be your lucky day," I said, leaning into the balloon, the only thing separating her from my raging hard-on.

Chapter 23

The devil's initial salvo was a rat-a-tat-tat of raindrops across our windshield, warning shots from a Gatling gun. The enemy letting us know they were near. The flurries continued. Rat-a-tat-tat. Rat-a-tat-tat. Morse code for 'Don't come any closer or we'll fuck you up.' I flicked on the windshield wipers and drove on. Unafraid. My mission: to get to Nicaragua as soon as humanly possible. I wouldn't be deterred.

The weather worsened with each click of the odometer, platoons of black goblins marching across the sky. We continued south, hugging the Pacific, as volleys of rain strafed the windshield. The splotches grew bigger, thick globs of translucent oil detonating across the glass. Heavier bursts landed, too, artillery shots making the Beast shudder and quake. But we refused to give up. The sun, moon, and stars faded away, drowned by slicks of jet-black oil. I was no longer a driver, but a mariner, steering our boat through a storm, waves crashing about our bow.

I drove through the night, through sheets of rain and howling winds, ignoring the danger that was licking at our heels. We still had a long road ahead. A week, maybe two, with this weather. But if I drove all day, and most of the night, I could cut that time in half. I just needed to keep driving. To continue moving.

But mother nature had her own plans, cranking up the rain and wind, and making it difficult to stay on course. Road signs disappeared, blended into the mush. Our map, useless in the dark. Forced to retrace our route, we peered into the black sludge, searching for offramps and exits as the roads deteriorated. The rain deconstructing them bit by bit, turning them into muddy, rutted pits. I was about to pull over and call it a night when the rain finally stopped. Sensing an opening, I pushed on, even though I'd been driving since 5 in the morning, and it was not pushing midnight.

Two hours later, while driving along an empty stretch of road, yawning, and shaking my head to stay awake, I spotted a series of tin cans lined up on either side of the road, flames flickering out of their center. It looked like some sort of landing strip, or clandestine meeting spot in the middle of nowhere. Something was up and I didn't care to find out what. I searched for an empty patch of dirt to pull into for the night, but the road had berms on either side. I slowed and crept forward, sensing danger. The road curved around a dune and came to a stop at a military checkpoint. An olive-green jeep parked just off the road had a menacing machine gun mounted to its top, its long barrel tracking us as we inched forward. My stomach was in my throat and my eyes, drawn to the flames dancing freely above the tin cans. Moving closer, the wind picked up, slashing at the flames and screaming, "Turn back, you stupid gringo!"

I came to a stop next to the jeep, where a boy in camouflage fatigues, who couldn't have been over 16 years old, poked his head inside the Beast and grunted, "*Papeles!*" Handing him our ream of documents, I noticed his eyes. They looked like burned oil, or tar, or the black hole storm we'd just passed through.

"*¿Que pasa?*" I asked, as he flipped through the papers for several minutes, hoping to break the tension and awkward silence.

He stared at me with those cold, dark pupils, an AK47 strapped to his back in an 'I don't take any fucking shit' manner, its muzzle poking up just above his left shoulder. I looked out the passenger-side window, just past Mari, and spotted another kid in fatigues peering in. His AK wasn't nestled safely on his back but cradled in his hands. Mari nudged closer, as I tried to figure out just what in the hell was going on.

"What's in the trailer?" the soldier demanded.

"Nothing," I replied, nervously. "Just some personal items. We're moving to Nicaragua." Just past him, an additional four or five soldiers were milling about on a berm next to the jeep.

He continued staring, his scowl growing deeper, then snapped, "Where are the drugs?"

"Drugs? I don't have any drugs!" I proclaimed. Although, at that moment, I probably would have sold a kidney for some drugs…Any drugs! Or booze…Any booze!

The guy next to Mari shuffled off toward the back of the truck, while my guy kept eyeing the trailer, glaring at it as if it was loaded down with cocaine.

"Out of the vehicle!" he said, slapping the door with his hand.

"You have no right to stop us," Mari said, before I could react, her voice traveling over my shoulder. "We're from the United States and have done nothing wrong."

"Shut up!" the soldier screamed, drops of his spit shooting across my cheek. My heart was racing, knowing that shit could go south at any moment. It was pitch black and nearing two in the morning on a lonesome road in Chiapas, Mexico. We were surrounded by Mexican soldiers not old enough to shave, with itchy fingers and AKs strapped to their backs, grilling us about drugs and contraband. This wasn't some Sancho Pancho sheriff shaking me down in his local town. No, I needed to do something, and fast!

"*Oye, oye, calmaté, calmaté*—Calm down, calm down," I began. "Look, friend, we're just trying to get to Nicaragua. I'm sure we can work this all out. We don't have any drugs. Can't we just pay some kind of toll? I mean, we're just *transportistas*, after all. See…" I pointed to the sticker plastered across our windshield, that abominable decal attracting cops to us like bees to honey. Army boy 1 stepped back and conferred with Army boy 2 while I fidgeted and squirmed in my seat. Minutes later, the dynamic duo returned, tar eyes leaning into my window and whispering, "*Veinte dólares.*"

"Twenty dollars!" Mari blared. I grabbed her arm and squeezed.

"Okay, no problem," I said, quickly, before he changed his mind.

Mari continued to mutter as I felt around for my wallet. We'd been shaken down plenty by then, but usually for only a dollar or two. This would be our highest ransom to date. But it sure in the hell beat emptying the trailer again. Or getting shot in the head on the side of some lonesome road in Chiapas.

So, after handing him a twenty-dollar bill, I actually thanked him. Thank you for allowing me to bribe you. He pointed two fingers to the south and took a step backward, while the other soldier tightened his gripped on his AK47. The machine gun perched atop the roof of the jeep swiveled and followed us as we drove away. Mari was still hot about having to cough up twenty bucks, but deep down, I think she was relieved. Through my mirror, I saw the flames in the tin cans one last time. They were waving as if to say goodbye, then disappeared into the night.

My adrenaline was still pumping, twenty miles down the road, when we finally found a spot to park hidden amidst a cluster of trees. My eyelids were as heavy as stones as I crawled into bed and listened to thunder booming in the distance, and the pitter patter of rain as it bounced off our roof. All I wanted was to close my eyes and disappear. But I couldn't help but smile, knowing that I was living my life. No longer in service to a time clock or subjugated by norms and ideals constructed before my time. No, not tonight. Or this morning. Or whatever fucking day this is. Nope, today I was a free man.

Chapter 24

We fell asleep to rain and awoke to rain, a steady downpour. A few miles up the road, we stopped at an outdoor food stall and ordered some breakfast from a sweet old lady. "Best be careful out there," she warned, handing us mugs of steaming hot coffee and plates of pastries. "Big storm's passing through Central America."

Central America? My ears perked up. I'd been hoping to make it there by day's end. Guatemala, anyway. Now, you would think a big storm passing through Central America would be cause for alarm. But I quickly dismissed it. Knowing that most storms that hit Central America originate in the Atlantic, churning up the sea as they move southwest, and occasionally veer into the Caribbean, where they make landfall on the Mosquito Coast of Nicaragua and Honduras. Once there, they quickly break apart, forming tropical depressions that deposit heavy rains across the Central American isthmus as they march toward the Pacific. This 'rainy season' is what keeps Central America so lush and green from April through December. Having lived through these storms and bouts of punishing rains, I brushed off her concerns. What did concern me, however, was that Mari—who'd lived her entire life in Nicaragua, not just a few like me—seemed worried.

"Don't worry, we'll be fine," I assured her, as rain splatted down on the blue tarp that served as a roof.

Once back on the road, I had to reassure myself that everything would be fine, as the Beast sloshed and banged through muddy roads and recently bulldozed detours that peeled off from the main highway. The constant deluge of rain was tearing up the roads, turning asphalt into taffy. But I kept going, determined to make it to the Guatemala border by day's end.

As evening approached, my shoulders and neck were in agony. Hunched forward, searching for road signs and markings that might point the way. The rain, unrelenting, was coming down in buckets, making the windshield wipers nearly useless as they struggled to keep up. Sensing the border was closed, I kept my foot on the gas.

A bolt of lightning shot across the sky, illuminating the dark night, followed by a deafening thunderclap that rattled the Beast. Quetzalcoatl, the Aztec God of life, was giving us a final sendoff. We'd made it through our rite of passage, passing through his ancestral land. A land not for the weak, but for the strong and the hearty.

He hurled a last shower of bolts across the sky, showcasing his power and the strength of his people. The sky lit up, ablaze in glory. And there, through the fog and dark and rain, was the Guatemalan border.

It was quiet, void of the usual bustle, with a string of cars and semis parked along the side of the road. We crept forward, making it to the front of the border, which was really just a long, metal bar painted yellow. The bar was down, blocking the road. There was no movement, nobody manning the border. "Where the hell is everybody?" I asked, putting the truck into park and looking around.

"Wait here," I told Mari, after tapping my fingers on the steering wheel for several minutes. I grabbed my rain jacket and hurried to the nearest building, where I found two chubby men leaning back in chairs, their feet propped up on a couple of desks.

"*Buenas*," I said, in my politest voice. "There's nobody in the booth out front."

They didn't even look up, just kept on reading their newspapers. "*Está cerrado por la tormenta*—It's closed because of the storm," one said.

"Closed! How can you close the border?"

The men ruffled their papers, visibly annoyed by the gringo invading their private time.

"So…when will it be open?"

"*Quién sabe*—Who knows," said the other, still not looking up.

I felt the blood rushing to my face. Whoosh! Whoosh! I'd been driving four, five…maybe six days by then. Who could really tell? It was all one big blur. I'd driven halfway across the United States, including Texas. Yes, Texas! Which goes on and on and on and on, seemingly forever! Been to practically every border crossing between San Diego and the Gulf of Mexico, only to be denied and sent on my way. Stopped and bribed from one end of Mexico to the other. Given up on my lifelong dream of surfing and fishing my way down

Mexico. And forced to drive like a madman through unrelenting rain to get to this very point. Now, these two dipshits are going to tell me I've reached the end of the line. Here, on the border of Guatemala and Mexico? Sorry, kid, game over. Thanks for playing.

Well, fuck that!

If I'd learned anything on this trip, so far, it was that there was always another way, an alternate course, a Plan B. If you tried sticking to your original plan, never deviating from it once, you'd break apart into a million pieces. Real life drops bombs on your head, dragging you down to your knees. It's down in that muck where we find our core. That inner, ballsy, side of us, that kicks fucking ass. That's when we react and counteract. Adjust and readjust. That's when we find the strength to move. Constantly move. Pushing forward.

Ever forward.

"*Oye, amigo*," I said, in my deepest voice. "I'm a United States diplomat and need to be in my post in Nicaragua in three days. You need to open the border immediately!"

I'm not sure where the idea came from, perhaps from watching my Peace Corps bosses blow through police checkpoints with their yellow, diplomatic license plates. But it seemed to do the trick, as the men hopped off their chairs and approached the counter. "*¿Cómo?*—What?" they asked, nervously.

"I said, I'm a U.S. diplomat," I repeated, then gave a little spiel about having to get to the Embassy in Managua, Nicaragua to deal with pressing matters.

"But, sir, the borders are all closed right now. Because of the storm. Nobody's allowed through."

Wait, did he just refer to me as sir? Making progress. "Now, listen," I continued, "it's extremely important that you let me through. The Nicaragua government is expecting me. Why is the border closed, anyway? Because of a storm? That's ridiculous."

The lead agent babbled on about the storm, and the order to close the border coming from above, how he was unauthorized to let us through. I realized, after several minutes of him repeating himself, that our conversation was leading nowhere. So, I adjusted, pivoted to Plan B.

"Look, friends, I know you have your orders, but what if I just paid an extra toll for you to let us through?"

Their eyes widened, and moments later, they were off in a corner whispering like thieves in the night. Returning to the counter, their eyes had that glint of bribery I'd seen so many times before. "Sir, since you need to get to Managua for official government business, we'll make an exception and let you through. But you'll have to come back at midnight, after the *jefe* is gone, and pay a special fee of $100."

A hundred fucking dollars! I wanted to scream, to jump over the counter and punch them in their faces. But I didn't. I remained calm, knowing there were no other options. *Forward, Kev. Forward.*

"Bueno," I said, in disgust.

He followed me back to the truck, rain pelting down, and glanced over the rig, before lifting the yellow bar so that I could make a U-turn and return to the Mexican side.

"$100? To cross the border…are you crazy? We can't afford that! We won't have any money left by the time we arrive in Nicaragua." Mari was pissed and letting me know it as I searched for a place to park.

"Well, what do you want to do?" I argued. "Sit here in this long ass line with all these freaking people and wait for the storm to pass? That could be days…maybe weeks. I just want to get the hell out of Mexico."

I was tired and hungry, and my body felt like it had been through a grinder. But the thought of sitting and waiting at the border, inside our cramped camper, seemed like torture. And after a few minutes, as the reality of our situation sunk in, Mari's anger subsided. She didn't want to wait in that line any more than I did. "Fine," she said, with a dip in her tone, as I pulled into a dirt lot. We sat back in our seats, watching the rain gush down the windshield, waiting for the bewitching hour to arrive.

Chapter 25

We raced to Jen's dorm, zigzagging across campus like balls in a pachinko machine, the night hot and sweaty, kamikazes oozing from our pores. We sped up near the student union, skipping and laughing, then broke into a jog as we crossed Big Chico Creek. The back-and-forth banter, the flirtation—faded away, leaving only raw animal attraction. Lust that needed to be satiated.

A single kiss had sealed our fate. An electric kiss that occurred just a short while ago, at GDI's *Get-to-Know-you* social, where college kids exercised their God Damn Independence.

After carefully situating the balloon between our chests, I wrapped my arms tight around Jen and squeezed, timidly at first, but then tighter. The balloon proved formidable, as if made from some super-strength latex just for us. I pulled Jen in closer and squeezed, but it still wouldn't pop. I moved the balloon higher on our breastplates. She laughed and adjusted her arms around my back, a sense of comradery growing between us. Then, with one last squeeze, a mighty bearhug, the balloon popped, thrusting us into each other's arms where neither of us seemed eager to leave. Thankfully, my erection had eased with all the concentration and effort put into completing our task. When we finally pulled apart, a note from inside the balloon floated to the ground.

I snatched it off the floor and pretended to read it. God only knows what it said. "It says to kiss your partner." Jen looked on hesitantly, her eyes dancing, questioning. Perhaps not so much me, but herself. Was this a road she wanted to travel? She tilted her head and closed her eyes; the answer was yes.

Her lips were fluffy, like pillows you lay your head on and never want to leave. The kiss grew, igniting a spark, as our tongues traveled farther and deeper, electricity coursing through our bodies. The energy, alive and palpable, and growing. Our fate, most definitely, sealed. We were having sex that night. The only question was how fast and in whose bed?

Nine minutes. That was the answer to the 'How fast?' question. The time it took for us to race through the streets of Chico, across campus, and into her dorm room. We left a trail of clothes from the door to her bed, tearing off bras and panties and boxers and flinging them into the air. Sliding inside her, the pressure was sheer pleasure. She twisted and squirmed as I licked her neck and nibbled on her ears. We grinded on each other harder and harder, sweat dripping off our chins. I pinned her hands above her head as she arched her hips and sighed in pleasure. Our tongues slid back and forth, stopping only for gasps of air. We were in a frenzy, our thirst unquenchable.

I would make that same late-night trek to Jen's dorm throughout my first year at Chico State, stumbling drunk and horny into her arms. Jen became my beacon, my lighthouse in the storm, letting me to crawl into her warm bed and disappear. Bright and funny and full of positivity, a rare amalgam. She made me want to stay which was odd, since I normally wanted to rip my arm off and sprint away the moment sex was over, uncomfortable in forming any deeper connection than a purely physical one. But with Jen, it was different. I could relax and talk about life and our hopes and dreams for the future. She was that special breed.

Yet, during all of our time together, I never learned to appreciate our budding relationship, or the uniqueness of Jen's personality. I was too young and stupid, too self-involved, to realize just how rare those electrical charges can be. Subsequently, I pulled away, moved in other directions.

Mostly, I pursued other women, as it wasn't the conquest that lit my fire, but the hunt. My primordial drive, buried deep within my brainstem, prevented me from settling down. I wasn't a nester, or a gatherer, or a farmer. I surely wasn't a boyfriend. No, I was a hunter.

***

Midnight approached, as Mari and I drove back to the border, neither of us saying a word. The rain continued unabated, turning the edges of the road into streams. We neared the yellow pole and waited. The border agent from earlier came out and waved us inside. Mari and I dashed through the rain and entered a dimly lit office.

"$100," he said, wasting little time. I pulled five twenties from my pocket and reluctantly handed them over. Once firmly in his grasp, he signaled to the other agent to stamp our passports, then led us to a building on the Guatemalan side, where yet another man stood waiting in the shadows. Inching closer, I wondered if we were about to be mugged. He stepped into the light, revealing a young, nonthreatening face. He requested $20 for the Guatemalan entry, which I readily gave, then set about filling out a series of immigration documents and stamping our passports. "You'll need these documents to leave Guatemala," he said, stapling the papers together and handing them to Mari. "But, if I were you, I'd find a place to stay nearby and wait out the storm. Honduras and Nicaragua are getting pretty hard."

"Bueno," I replied, knowing full well I would not stop. I was on a mission. I could see Mari looking at me through my peripheral vision, seeking reassurance. But I kept my head trained forward, not wanting to lose focus. Not wanting to lose my nerve. A guard raised the yellow pole and let us through, as rain hammered down, the Beast's windshield wipers scraping rivers of water off the glass.

Less than a quarter mile into Guatemala, I missed the turnoff for the highway, and ended up on the outskirts of a small town. The electricity must have been out as it was pitch black, not a single light to be found.

"Turn here!" Mari shouted. But it was too late. We were driving down a narrow road which I suspected might be a dead end. My fears only increased as we neared the end, hoping and praying for an alley or sideroad to emerge and lead us out of this mess. Knowing there was no way in hell I could turn our rig around on such a narrow pass. And forget about reversing, as I'd learned from recent experience that it was virtually impossible to back up the trailer without jackknifing it every ten yards because of its small size in relation to the truck.

The inevitable arrived as we reached the end of the dark street. A dead end. Nowhere to go. Mari shook her head in disgust. My anger rose like a shot of helium in my veins. *How could I be so fucking stupid?*

I slammed the Beast into park and stewed. Turning around was impossible, and there was no way I could back all the way down that long-ass road, especially with our trailer, which had a mind of its own. I plumbed the jagged contours of my mind, searching for an answer to the riddle. The solution: unhook the trailer and roll it off to the side, then attempt to turn the truck around inside the narrow road. It was the only way.

A mixture of hope and pessimism filled me as I trudged to the back of the truck, drenched in rain, and fiddled with the trailer hitch. I quickly realized I'd need a hammer to pry it free and made my way inside the camper. I felt around for my toolbox, digging among the boxes and bins as water drained off me. I found it behind a stack of boxes and returned to the trailer, banging on the hitch with both a hammer and a crowbar. The noise attracted a group of teenagers who came over and stood behind me. "*¡Oye, gringo,* we can help you!"

"No, that's ok," I said, rapping ever harder on the metal hitch.

"Come on, just let us help you," they repeated.

Brushing the rain off my face, I wedged the crowbar between the hitch and the ball and cranked on it with all my might. It creaked and groaned, then gave up the fight, releasing the trailer from the truck. But the battle was only half won. I still needed to lift the trailer and roll it to the side of the road. I squatted down into the dead-lift position, clutched the trailer by its collar and lifted with all my might. Nothing. Straining under all the weight, I let out a roar and cranked up again, using my legs and my arms. But the trailer wouldn't budge. Not one fucking inch.

More teenagers arrived, forming a semicircle, as they eyed me curiously, rain beating down on their heads. They looked bewildered, wondering, perhaps, why this stupid gringo was alone, in this dark alley in the middle of the night.

I tried one last time to lift the trailer, squaring up my shoulders and digging my flip-flops into the mud. I lifted with everything I had, but the trailer wouldn't budge. I looked over my shoulder at the small crowd that had amassed and relented. "*Bueno, ayudame.*" A moment later, eight teenage boys, seemingly impervious to the rain, gathered around the trailer and lifted it off the ground. "Okay, un momento, un momento," I said, racing back to the truck and driving forward.

With my clothes sopping wet, I turned the truck and then quickly reversed, as the boys rolled the trailer to the side of the road and rested it on the ground. The Beast crept forward a few feet more, then reversed a few feet, repeating the process over and over. Stopping just before we hit a building or brick wall. This back-and-forth madness went on for a good twenty minutes, with Mari using a towel to wipe the rain and sweat off my face, as I attempted a hundred-point turn, bitching and moaning the entire way. The humidity was through the roof, and by the time I got the truck turned around, I was sweating from every orifice in my body.

Walking back to the trailer, the rain came as a relief, washing away my sweat. The boys huddled around and stared, awaiting their next orders. The crowd had swelled, at least twenty deep, some as young as five or six years old—brothers and sisters of the teenagers. I told my crew to get the trailer and bring it back to the truck. They all pitched in, swinging the trailer in a wide arc, and dragging it up the street.

I wondered, for a moment, as they wheeled the overloaded trailer up the road, if they might roll it away altogether. Turn down some hidden alley and disappear in the night. I almost hoped they would abscond with that godforsaken trailer. But, oh, what great sadness there would be, after prying off the lock and discovering their new treasure: a collection of rusty tools, worn-out sports equipment, and boxes of random, worthless crap. And books. Stacks and stacks of books, all in English. I could almost feel their despair.

"*¡Gringo, gringo!*" the crowd beckoned, as I pushed my way to the back of the truck, where they had the trailer perfectly aligned over the metal ball. Sadly, I wouldn't be leaving the trailer behind in this blacked-out town on the border of Guatemala.

A flurry of hands help lower the trailer onto the ball, adjusting it into place, and then clamping down the lock. After plugging in the brake lights, a silence fell over the crowd, as forty eager eyes were upon me. Suddenly, they all shouted, "*¡Gringo, gringo, regalame un peso! Regalame un peso!*" Hands were shoved in my face from every direction. "Give us some money! Give us some money! For helping you!" I stood, and the crowd closed around me. A chill raced down my spine when I couldn't make it back to the truck.

"Okay, okay, but you need to back up first," I pleaded with the crowd. "My money is in the truck." They created a narrow path which I bolted through like a linebacker in an open field. "Lock your door!" I ordered Mari, jumping inside the truck, and quickly locking my own. My hands were shaking as I jiggled the key into the ignition and fired up the Beast. The crowd slapped at the windows and banged on the doors as I eased away. One boy latched onto the side-view mirror and lifted himself off the ground, while others hopped on the trailer hitch. "Grab my wallet," I told Mari, cautiously rolling down my window a few inches. I pulled out a wad of dollar bills and the last of our Mexican pesos and shoved them out the window. The boy clutching my window released his grip and chased after the money. The rest of the crowd soon followed, sprinting through the rain, and catching bills mid-flight while I punched the gas and got the hell out of Dodge.

Chapter 26

Jen and I fell into a strange, quasi-relationship that first year at Chico State, always seeming to find each other at the end of alcohol-fueled Friday and Saturday nights, after party hopping and sneaking into bars, her on one side of Chico and me on the other, the magnetic draw too strong to resist. We were both night owls and our rendezvouses took place late at night—one, two, three o'clock in the morning—providing an added allure, like secret lovers in an illicit affair.

The sex remained raw and fevered. No matter how many times we ripped each other's clothes off and dissolved into hot, sweaty pretzels, our desires— base and animalistic—never waned. I needed her body. Craved it. Sought it. Pursued it. Relentlessly. I was a fiend.

But I was emotionally stunted—a child, really—incapable of moving our relationship into something more serious. Something more substantial. And since Jen didn't seem to mind the Frankenstein relationship we'd cobbled together, or so I thought. So, I saw no point in changing it. Besides, the time spent after sex was just as fulfilling—laughing and joking about the mundane and absurd as we lied in bed naked and vulnerable. I craved that just as much as I did the sex. The friendship. The companionship.

I wonder, sometimes, if all that raw animal lust was just a shield, preventing me from getting close, from opening myself up to the pain that comes with love. And that crushing pain when it's ripped away. Yet that same shield that protects me, keeps me locked inside, a prisoner within, preventing me from reaching those far-off worlds where pretense dissolves and humanity rules. A land of calm and self-reflection. A neutral territory, where my evolutionary drive to breed and procreate is rewired—dimmed—just long enough to see the beauty in another being. To see their aura. To see Jen's beauty. To see Jen's aura…

Inevitably, those feelings would ebb, and I'd be pulled back into the genetic hunt. Primal instincts kicking in, reminding me of my prime objective: to continue my genetic line. And soon, my eyes were darting from female to female. Searching. My DNA pulling me in all directions, commanding me to spread my seed far and wide. Fucking with my head. Fucking with my sanity. Relinquishing its talons only when I'd finished the act.

***

Rain pounded down as we drove through Guatemala. Heaven unzipped her belly and released her power: atom bombs of thunder and javelins of lightning. And rain. Rain, rain, rain, rain. Dumping everywhere. The entire Pacific Ocean. Washing out entire stretches of freeway, pavement and all. We pulled over and watched her flex her muscles. Raw power rocking the Beast from side to side.

We hurried back to the camper, getting soaked along the way, then crawled into bed and cowered as the world exploded around us. Maybe that border agent was right. This wasn't some ordinary, run-of-the-mill Caribbean storm. This was some serious shit! I closed my eyes and tried to doze, as a symphony of crashing water and earsplitting thunder played above. Mozart lulling me to sleep.

We left early the next morning, the rain still coming down, only the thunder and lightning had ceased. The roads were horrendous, forcing us to drive in a snake-like fashion, winding around mudslides and giant craters that seemed intent on swallowing us up. Orange signs appeared every few miles that said '*Desvio*' with arrows pointing to muddy sideroads and offramps, where the freeway was no longer passable or completely washed out. Bulldozers were busy ripping down trees and carving out roads around these stretches. Some detours were short, maybe a hundred yards while others went on for miles. We drove on one particularly nasty road for over three hours with mud over a foot deep! The Beast roared like a lion as she picked her way through the rocky sludge, the trailer banging up and down like an angry child, and the camper teeter-tottering perilously from side to side.

The constant swaying and rocking caused one of the trailer brackets to rupture. The brackets, which were connected to four turnbuckles, secured the camper to the truck. Thankfully, the camper stayed on long enough for us to find another '*Se Vulcaniza,*' where the mechanic told us our best option was to weld the brackets directly to the truck, in order to prevent the camper from falling off or breaking part as we traveled over the rough roads that lay ahead. But it came with a risk: if the camper toppled over, it would drag the truck over with it.

I gave him the green light. Soon, sparks were flying as he welded the four brackets to the bed of the truck, making them permanent features on the Beast. When he finished, we continued slogging through the mud bog, tires spinning, spraying mud in all directions, the camper rocking hard from side to side. I stuck my arm out the window and braced my hand against the camper, as if I could prevent it from going over. As if I had a say in the direction it wished to go.

Then, just ahead, I saw asphalt. Precious asphalt. My heart filled with joy, knowing our twenty-kilometer detour through hell was ending. We stopped for diesel. While pumping gas under a leaky awning, the attendant warned us about the storm hitting Nicaragua and Honduras. He said it was bad, but I couldn't see how much worse it could be than the fucking tsunami we were currently driving through. He said that a lot of the highways along the Pacific had been destroyed, completely washed away, and the only way through was over the mountains.

Mari and I pulled out our trusty map and plotted a new course through the Sierra de los Cuchumatanes Mountains, unaware it was the highest non-volcanic mountain range in Central America, with peaks reaching over 12,500 feet.

Night came on fast, though you might not have known it by the black skies and heavy rain draping over everything like a black hole swallowing the stars. I moved closer to the windshield, attempting to see the road cleared, wipers thumping back and forth, pushing buckets of water off the glass. Darkness enveloped us as we began our ascent, save for the headlights shining but a few feet ahead. The Beast grunted and kicked into a lower gear as we rose higher into the night sky. I shuddered as wisps of fog appeared in the headlights. Then more fog came, crowding in around us like a new friend. I scooted closer to the windshield, my neck and shoulders throbbing in pain. The fog and rain combined, forming a heavy soup. I drove slowly, and moved so close to the windshield, I could see my breath on the glass. The temperature dropped, sending a chill through my body, clinging to my spine. I looked out the window, my neck fused to my shoulders. Fog and rain. Fog and rain. It was all just fog and rain.

"Can you see anything?" I asked Mari in desperation as we banked around a hairpin curve. Through a break in the fog, I saw the edge of a cliff. Pulling the steering wheel around, the headlights lit up the curve, revealing a steep drop, presumably thousands of feet down, to some bloodthirsty spot at the bottom of the Cuchumatanes Mountains. I needed to keep my shit together, or we'd find ourselves in that very spot, buried under the Beast, the camper, and a thousand pounds of books. "Well, they were well read…" the coroner would say.

A roar, like a runaway locomotive, came up from behind, followed by a foghorn blast that sent me jumping out of my seat. I peered into my side-view mirror as a pair of bright lights came speeding toward us. The devil had opened his gate, sending demons streaming forth. The lights got brighter, nearly blinding me, while the blaring horns sent shock waves through my inner ear. I pulled the truck to the edge of the road, just inches away from sudden death, the devil in hot pursuit as we climbed into the sky. The horn blasted again, then the lights were at our side. I kept my eyes on the road, trained on the sliver of dirt preventing us from hurtling off the cliff. But when the foghorn blared again, right next to me, I stole a glance at the devil. Apparently, he drove an 18-wheeler, as one blew past us at top speed, disappearing around a bend. My eyes returned to the road, which I was putt-putting along on at less than ten miles-per-hour, my nose pressed tight against the chilly windshield, wondering why there wasn't one fucking guardrail on the entire mountain.

We'd entered Mayan territory, who believed life was more than just a hodgepodge of events: birth, survival, struggle, toil, death. That life was about balance and harmony, respecting nature and taking only that which you need from it. The original explorers, they'd traveled across the entire planet to arrive at this very land I now traversed. You could almost hear their heartbeats echoing through the trees.

I let out a sigh as we crested the mountain peak. The Beast shifted gears and began the long descent into the foggy valley below. The rain continued but felt more like a healing as if opening a fresh path for Mari and me. Perhaps we'd absorbed a touch of the Mayan, forever moving forward. Progressing. Searching for that part inside that makes us unique. That core treasure which defines our humanity, fueling our fires, and seeking answers to those lofty questions: *Why are we here? What is our purpose?*

Chapter 27

I chugged beer from a Big Gulp cup held in one hand while firmly gripping Jen's steering wheel with the other. My junior year at Chico State had come and gone, and I was heading to Yosemite National Park where I'd applied and received a job for the summer. Jen had graciously volunteered to give me a lift into the Sierra Nevada Mountains, although, by that point, as I drank beer and listened to the new U2 cassette on a loop, she might have been regretting that decision. The job couldn't have come at a better time, as I was about as broke as a person could be, barely two nickels to rub together after my latest beer purchase. But I'd be living in God's country soon. Or so I'd been told. As I'd never actually been to Yosemite. But, then again, I'd never been to a lot of places.

"You, sure you're, okay?" Jen asked, as I steered through the mountain curves.

"Hell, yeah!" I replied, handing her the Big Gulp cup.

She took a sip of beer and grimaced, "Yuck!"

"Yuck? That's nectar of the Gods."

"More like warm piss of the Gods. Hey, maybe I should drive, Mr. Nectar boy."

"No way."

We entered a long tunnel dug into the side of a mountain. Fluorescent lights flickered overhead, illuminating the vast cavern as we drove on and on, the tunnel seemingly endless. But then daylight flooded in, and we emerged on the other side, into the most breathtaking sight I'd ever seen. The Garden of Eden. After pulling over, Jen and I raced to the edge of a cliff and stared out at the majestic Yosemite Valley, her beauty and grandeur leaving us in awe. Granite monoliths rose into the clouds as a massive waterfall poured into the valley below. A valley of green that stretched as far as the eyes could see. This really was God's country.

"Wow!" Jen said. "This truly is amazing, and just think, you'll be living here for an entire summer. I'm so jealous."

"You should be," I teased. "Because this is my land now." I stretched out my arms wide. "Now, come and I will show you more." Jen rolled her eyes as I held out my hand and motioned for her to follow me back to the car.

Jen and I arrived in Curry Village, in a pine forest valley just below Half Dome and Glacier Point, two massive granite mountains. We followed a trail of pine needles to the Orientation Office. After filling out some final paperwork, they handed me a key to a wood-framed tent where I'd be living for the next three months. Yosemite was now home.

Jen and I went to check out my new digs. The tent, which they'd be deducting $13 per week in rent from my check, was rather basic: wood plank floors and framing covered by a canvas roof and walls. A springy metal bed sat in the corner, with a thin mattress covered in old, green army blankets. It was about as barebones as you could get. I threw my backpack on the bed, then Jen and I set off to explore the valley floor. Half Dome poked its head out over the valley, a watchman guarding all. While El Capitan, 'the captain,' stood tall and proud on the other side of the valley, reaching 7,500 into the air. The Merced River twisted and turned below, through meadows and trees, forming a sanctuary for the many birds and deer and other wildlife that called Yosemite home that lived within this veritable paradise.

Later that evening, as Jen and I lay in the springy bed, listening to birds chirping, and insects buzzing and clicking, nature in its purest state, I felt a mounting excitement for the summer ahead. Yet with it came a strange sadness, knowing that Jen wouldn't be there to experience it. She was leaving in the morning. Our relationship had never progressed. We were friends and lovers, a non-committal mishmash just as barebones and empty as the tent I now lived within. Yet, this hollow feeling gnawing away on my insides made me question whether there wasn't something more to us. Something worth clinging onto.

A summer would now pass between us with each of us exploring the world in our own unique way. What would remain at the end of those three months? Will the bridge connecting us together still stand? Or will it have crumbled, disintegrated, leaving only a chasm as deep and as wide as the Yosemite Valley between us?

Jen rested her head on my chest, her heat radiating to my core. I pressed her close, knowing the moment was fleeting, knowing she would soon be gone, along with her warmth, absorbed into the meadows and streams of Yosemite. God's land. We kissed gently, our love, built upon layers of sand, left in the hands of fate.

The following morning was frosty. Walking Jen to her car, the sun's rays ricocheted off granite slabs. I wrapped my arms around her and squeezed. How long could we push our luck? How long could we dance around the edge of love without falling off the cliff?

"Hey," Jen said, grabbing my chin and centering our eyes. "Don't waste this opportunity. There's a reason you're here."

"I won't."

"You better not, or I'll hunt you down."

"Hmm…sounds like fun."

"I'm serious."

"Okay, okay…I'll follow in John Muir's footsteps, and the next time you see me, I'll be one with nature. A true transcendentalist."

"Don't get lost up there in the mountains, nature boy. Some of us might miss you."

A pang ripped through my spleen as she drove away, leaving me all alone in the valley of heaven.

But I wouldn't be alone for long. As Yosemite, a magical land with infinite possibilities, quickly became my companion that summer. I cleaned tourist cabins and tents in the morning, then by early afternoon, I was free to explore. After hiking all the main trails, I discovered remote trails and hidden waterfalls. Each day posed a new challenge, a new adventure: swimming in the Merced River, climbing rocks and trees, hiking to the peaks of mountains, or just getting lost in a meadow.

I thought about life on these adventures. My life, in particular, and where I fit in the broader context. One couldn't help but feel small and inconsequential while standing next to those towering granite megaliths. But that granite contained a great well of power within its core. A power to imbue strength and character, empathy, and knowledge, to those willing to listen and absorb its lessons, for those willing to transcend. Yosemite took me under its wing that summer, kneading and molding me into something new. Something more. Sculpting me into a man.

Yet the questions still lingered. Where did I fit into this complex world? What was my role? There just had to be something more to life, something deeper and more profound than this blasé existence bestowed upon me by some previous civilization. But no matter how much I searched within Yosemite's towering majesty, amidst its unbridled beauty, its richness and complexity, through its diversity and its peace—the answers remained elusive, fluttering in the wind just beyond my grasp.

So, I did what any other red-blooded 21-year-old would do: drank and partied and went back on the hunt. Chasing women, who—between the tourists and co-workers—were in abundance. Jen quickly faded from my mind as the tourists came and went. A new fling every week. No commitments. Perfect. We'd have sweaty sex in the meadow in the middle of the day, the four-foot-high grass hiding our naked bodies. At night, we'd trek deep into the woods, with only the moon as our guide, then build a bonfire and drink Vodka, before making love in a patch of soft dirt, under a sea of stars, while owls hooted, and coyotes howled.

I became friends with a few co-workers, who also enjoyed hiking. And by the end of the summer, we'd hiked nearly every trail in Yosemite, including most of the backcountry. We'd even made it to the top of Half Dome, which had been peering down at us all summer long. There were only two weeks left in the season, and all of us were eager to return to college or home and resume our old lives. I'd only spoken to Jen twice over the summer. And I missed her. A lot.

But then a fire broke out on the outskirts of the valley, and within hours, smoke covered the valley floor. By the next day, they had ordered all the tourists to evacuate. We didn't have access to TVs, so all of our information was sporadic. Rumors quickly spread that the fire was heading toward us, but management ordered all employees to stay put and await further instructions. By the following day, the skies had turned dark orange and a smoky haze engulfed Yosemite. The animals fled overnight, leaving the valley eerily silent. I decided it was time to leave, especially after learning the park had ceased all sales of alcohol. That was a bridge too far.

My boss, a haughty lady who never hid her disdain for us 'short timers' or 'college brats,' told us that under no circumstance were we to leave the valley. And that we were still under contract with Curry Village. So, when my buddy, Tommy, pulled up in his van and told me he was getting the hell out of there,

I promptly told her to 'Fuck off!' Adding some mumble jumble about not being an indentured servant while pointing out the obvious: Yosemite was on fire. Hello! And did I mention they'd stopped selling beer?

We drove as fast as the van would take us down the last highway still open. Smoke poured into the van, becoming so thick we had to soak our bandanas and t-shirts in water and wrap them around our faces. The sun disappeared, faded into the black-and-orange haze. Moments later, flames appeared on the ridges above us, coming closer the farther we drove. We thought about turning around and going back, but it was too late for that. Soon, the flames were on both sides of the van, leaping twenty feet in the air, the heat radiating through the metal frame like a blowtorch. Flames shot across the road, slashing at the van like a devil smacking his whip. Tommy punched the gas while I sat on the edge of my seat, pulse racing, black smoke and flames billowing across our path. The metal inside the van became too hot to the touch. I wondered how long it would be before the tires melted, leaving us stranded in the middle of the fire.

But then, through the smoke, I saw something on the horizon. "Look!" I screamed, pointing to an opening in the haze. You could just make out the contours of the sun. Light at the end of the tunnel—literally. Minutes later, we were out of the fire. We whooped and hollered and gave high fives, then headed to the nearest liquor store. We learned later that the winds shifted, sparing Yosemite and its workers.

Yosemite taught me to embrace life and nature and find harmony within. Perhaps I hadn't found my purpose yet. But, at the very least, I was heading in the right direction. I also realized that I loved Jen. And I would tell her the moment I saw her next.

Chapter 28

Guatemala was drenched, waterlogged. The rain coming down hard and unabated. By my calculations, it had been raining for four days straight. Nonstop, continuous inundation. But Mari and I drove on, through the rain and the fog, the lightning and thunder—not the slightest glimmer of easing. We made it down the Cuchumatanes Mountains and back onto the main highway, only to be met with more of the dreaded detours, forcing us to roll through muddy roads, weaving in and around swollen rivers and bucked highway.

The Beast squeaked and grumbled, and swayed from side to side at precarious angles, while I, instinctively, stupidly, reached my hand through the window and braced it against the camper. As if I had some superhuman strength to prevent it from toppling over, Atlas holding up the world. The rain didn't give a shit about our plight. It just kept coming. Taunting us. Noah's Ark type rain that saturated the land. The Beast was our lifeboat, now, and I, it's captain. All I needed was my fucking rum!

A sign appeared through the black, watery haze. 'El Salvador.' We'd made it to yet another border—where, once again, a bright yellow pole blocked our passage. Our truck was the only vehicle in line, as if the entire world had been swallowed up.

"*Está cerrado*-It's closed," a voice called out. A chubby border agent appeared through the fog, draped in a yellow poncho, and walking with a slight limp.

"*¿Cerrado?*" I was having déjà vu all over.

He pointed to the sky and muttered, "The storm. Everything's closed because of the storm." But before I could complain, he hobbled off, disappeared into a wooden shed, which was nearly invisible through the rain and mist.

I gave Mari a familiar glance, then jumped out of the truck. I didn't even stop at the shed, just pressed on to the main building, where the word '*Inmigración*' was painted above the door in big, white letters.

I rolled out my diplomat story to the man in charge, feeding him the same bullshit about having to get to my post in Managua ASAP. He looked me up and down. Sizing me up. Perhaps, I should've dressed the part, as my shorts and flip-flops inspired little confidence. He sneered and asked to see my credentials. I pulled out my old Peace Corps ID, hoping he wouldn't know the difference. He stared at it for a moment, then tossed it on the counter and raised his voice, "Nobody is allowed into El Salvador until the storm has cleared. All the borders from Mexico to Panama are closed. No exceptions."

"But, sir, I must get to the embassy in Managua. The ambassador is expecting me."

He turned and walked back to his chair. I was just a peon. A nobody. An insignificant pest interrupting the flow. "Wait a minute, can't I just pay an extra fee so that you can process us through?"

He turned back and took a new look at me. Undoubtedly assessing my ability to pay. Perhaps I wasn't a peon after all, that I was more than my beach bum attire might denote. It was fairly obvious I wasn't going to any embassy, but perhaps I had a few bills tucked inside those board shorts.

"What are you driving?" he scowled.

"A truck," I replied, smiling inwardly. "We're at the gate."

He came around the counter and poked his head out the door, peering at our truck and trailer, barely visible through the rain and mist.

"A hundred dollars," he said emphatically. "And we'll need to go through your possessions to ensure there are no drugs or contraband." He pointed to a large bay with a tin roof. "Pull in over there."

Mari and I spent the next two hours pulling out all our boxes and lining them up on a cement slab, while a group of men rummaged through our mismatched silverware, chipped plates, ratty clothes, and rusty saws. My face turned red with shame, looking at all the junk spread out in one location for all the world to see. This giant conglomeration of crap which I'd been lugging across state lines and through multiple countries. Even the agents snickered at my cacophony of shit.

Mari stared in disbelief at the random assortment of junk, seeing it all now for the first time. She glanced at me from time to time, but I looked away each time. The only saving grace was the fact that we were definitely not hoarding any drugs or contraband. The rain crashed down on the tin roof above us, drowning out the agents' laughs and sighs as they opened up more boxes of trash.

"Okay, put it all back," the lead agent finally said.

I wondered, while stacking boxes back inside the camper, why I'd brought so much 'stuff' as if we were moving to some remote, uninhabited place for the rest of our lives. We weren't. We were moving to Pueblo Nuevo, a small town in the mountains of northern Nicaragua. There were stores there, even a couple of restaurants. Why had I packed as if we'd just survived the Battle of Armageddon?

Money, I suppose. Fourteen thousand dollars is a pittance. Yet, that fourteen thousand dollars was supposed to see us through for the rest of our lives. Or, rather, tide us over until we opened a business. If, after arriving in Nicaragua, we had to immediately begin buying fresh supplies, our little nest egg would quickly disappear. So, while bringing rusty hammers and chipped plates might seem idiotic to some, if not all, to me it meant the difference between making it in Nicaragua or not. And I sure as shit didn't want to go back to the U.S.

The boss man came over and collected his hundred dollars, then motioned for somebody to raise the yellow pole. *¡Bienvenidos a El Salvador!*

Chapter 29

Chico is beautiful in the fall, a medley of color from the trees lining the streets. The familiar scent of Cedar, Spruce and pear trees greeted me, as students scampered about, talking excitedly as they moved suitcases and furniture into dorms and apartments. It was hot, and the humidity clung to my skin like a layer of cellophane. But I didn't mind. Chico was like an old friend, comfortable and safe. A friend that, no matter how long it had been since you saw them, you could pick up exactly where you left off. Yet something felt different this time. Something was off.

My stomach turned into a gymnast that first week of school, flipping and twisting, somersaulting, and cartwheeling. I searched for Jen, eager to tell her about Yosemite and my 'self-discovery.' To tell her how I wanted her in my heart. To show her I was no longer the same cool and aloof boy she'd dropped off in Yosemite months prior. I didn't want to play silly games anymore. I was ready to jump into this love thing headfirst. Ready to open up. To be myself, regardless of the pain it would expose me to.

Two days later, I spotted her, sitting under a sprawling sycamore tree, reading a syllabus. My heart felt like it was racing down a zipline as I approached. "Hey…"

"There you are!" She flashed a gigantic smile. "I was wondering when I'd see you. How was your summer?"

"Uh…" I mumbled. I thought about everything I wanted to tell her. But the words were all scrambled in my head. I tried to put them back in the correct order so that I could reveal the emotionally evolved man I'd become. A man that could profess his love right there in front of Lassen Hall. But the word 'Great' was all I could come up with, reverting to the neanderthal I'd always been. Yosemite's mystical power was fading fast, in real time, before my very eyes. "Hey, Jen…I…um…I wanted to say. Well, I wanted to tell you…Aw, shit, sorry, how was your summer?" *How was your summer? Bro, are you fucking kidding me?*

She looked on pensive. "Well, my summer was a blast. I interned for that marketing company I told you about, remember? Great experience, and right on the beach. I roller-bladed to work each day down the Redondo boardwalk. And I could spend a lot of time with my parents, which was nice. But wait, tell me all about Yosemite. It must have been amazing living there?" She looked at my worn-out Vans and the holes on the sides. "Looks like you got a lot of hiking in over the…"

"I missed you, Jen!" I blurted out, before my brain could resume the hostage situation it had me in.

Jen adjusted her head back. "Well, I missed you too…"

"No, I mean, I *really* missed you."

"Umm, it's a little early in the day to be drinking, don't you think?"

"No, Jen, I…" I tried, once again, to unravel the little spiel that was spinning inside my head. The one about wanting her in my life. About wanting something more for us. But I froze. Petrified of her reaction.

"You sure you haven't been drinking?" she said with a smile. "You usually only get emotional after seven beers. Or is it eight?"

"I'm serious, Jen, I missed you."

"Okay, okay. I missed you, too. You wouldn't believe how boring the guys are in Palos Verdes. Well, hey, I've got to get to class…" She jumped to her feet and swung on her backpack. "Let's talk over the weekend…" Then she rushed off like I had the Bubonic Plague.

Sweat dripped off my chin. Chico was much hotter than I'd remembered. I stared at my shoes, the same ones I'd worn while hiking throughout Yosemite. God's country. Where I'd learned I had value. That I was much more than my genetic substrate. More than just a chain of molecules. Yes, I was unique. An individual. With free thought and free will.

Chico hadn't changed. I had changed.

***

The Beast's big, burly tires with extra thick tread, known as 'mudders,' had proven themselves time and time again, having spent the better portion of the trip driving through mud bogs and mud pits. El Salvador was more of the same, as torrential rains had destroyed large swaths of their infrastructure. And while the truck's tires were holding up well, banging from one detour to another, the trailer was a different story entirely. And thirty miles past the border, it broke yet another weld. We found our way to a 'Se Vulcaniza,' then quickly ducked out of the rain, finding shelter under a palm-thatched roof, where we watched sparks ricochet off a welder's shield.

After finishing the welds, the owner looked over the trailer's tires, which, after being filled with the hardening agent, were like round lumps of cement. In a rare stroke of luck, he had two tires that were the same size as our old ones. The only problem was that the hubs were for a five-lug setup and our trailer only had four. "No problem," he said, pushing down his welding shield. "I can fix that." He set about welding a plate on the rim and drilling out new holes to fit the lugs. I thought about how ingenious the people were down here. Literally, able to fix anything, modify anything. Get you back on the road.

Merging back onto the Pan American Highway, I was met with a rare surprise: the freeway system running through El Salvador was both modern and in pretty decent shape, especially as we got closer to the capital of San Salvador. I wanted to speed through the country as fast as possible, overjoyed by the feel of smooth asphalt under the Beast, but the heavy rain and fog made for poor visibility. We stopped at a small stand on the side of the road and ate *pupusas*, a local favorite made from corn masa formed into a pancake then stuffed with pork, beef, chicken, cheese, olives, beans, onions, and other fillings. After cooking on a grill, they drizzle red or green sauce over the top for an extra kick. Mari and I stuffed our bellies full, then drove into a parking lot on the edge of town to sleep for the night.

The rain continued. This constant deluge becoming a part of our lives now. As if it had always rained and always would rain. This steady river, as consistent as the air we breathed and the blood pumping through our hearts. It was our companion now. A fellow traveler. Always there, in the periphery, coursing along. Carving its own path.

Mari massaged my neck and shoulders. Driving fifteen hours a day through blinding rain was kicking my ass. Our happy little 'vacation' had turned into a battle. A rite of passage. A test of strength and wills. The other side doing all it could to defeat me. To break me. To crumble me into a million pieces and send me scampering back to the United States—forever a shattered man. Mari continued to knead my shoulders, using her elbows to break up the knots. The pain only reinforced my resolve. I wouldn't let this fucker beat me. Uh, huh, no way. And there was no way in hell I was turning back!

We motored through El Salvador at a steady clip, the smooth pavement like a godsend after the nightmare roads of Mexico and Guatemala. And before long, we were pulling up to the border of Honduras.

"The border is closed," came the familiar words. Only this time, they gave us a new piece of information. The agent told us that Nicaragua and Honduras were getting blasted, not just by a powerful storm, but by a hurricane. And it had a name.

After forming in the western Caribbean Sea, it raced across the, Sea strengthening into a category five hurricane, before smashing into the east coast of Honduras. Then it slowed, moving at a snail's pace inland before stopping and sitting directly above southern Honduras and northern Nicaragua—the same spot we were headed. And for nearly a week, Hurricane Mitch had been sucking up water from the Pacific Ocean and dumping it on the land, causing massive flooding, destroying homes, and ripping up roads and bridges.

"*Que Dios bendiga a nuestro pobre país*—May God bless our poor country," the border agent said, making the sign of the cross and kissing the back of his thumb.

Maybe we shouldn't be bribing my way into Honduras, I thought. Into the apocalypse! Perhaps the more prudent decision would be to turn back and seek shelter, ride out the storm from afar. But Mari was eager to get home and check on her family who lived in the direct path of Mitch. And I…well, I was hellbent on completing the mission. On moving forward.

"*Soy un diplomático*," I proclaimed, my story well-polished by then. More importantly, I knew exactly when to offer the bribe—it's all in the delivery. Thirty minutes later, our passports were stamped, and we were ready to roll. "Careful out there, my friend, it's very dangerous," said the agent, as he cranked up the yellow pole, the last barrier separating us from the hell beyond. "*¡Cuidate!*" he repeated as we drove past, his eyes traveling over us like bumps on a sheet of braille.

Hurricane Mitch wasted little time in making its presence known, the skies howling and whistling and swirling about. Pale grays turned to inky blacks, before an earsplitting crack echoed overhead. A symphony of sledgehammers followed, banging away on metal gongs. Then the skies opened up, the entire

Pacific Ocean raining down. Hurricane Mitch was a monster, slamming into Earth with such ferocity, it revealed man for what he truly was: an insignificant speck in the Universe.

We pulled over and watched Mitch bare its fangs, cowering in our seats, as we peeked inside the bowels of hell. Mitch screamed, railing at the top of its lungs, pounding his fists upon the land, destroying all within its path. Its fury absolute. The Beast shook and trembled. I held Mari close, fearing that at any moment Mitch might pick us up and fling us like a pebble into the tempest.

But just when all hope seemed lost, and the world was about to fold up on itself; when humanity was nearing its climax, fading into the annals of history—a mere blip on the Earth's timeline; just when all life was about to cease, to be no more, Hurricane Mitch let out a last roar, a grand finale, rattling the sky and the ground, then fell silent.

Only the pitter patter of rain remained. A light drizzle. The war of the Gods was over. Mari peeked out from under my arm. We surveyed the battlefield, trying to make sense of what we'd just witnessed. But it's impossible to explain the inexplicable. All we really knew for sure was that we'd been driving through this thermonuclear storm for days and days. And that the last hurrah, the *coup de grace*, the *aria di bravura*, had taken place here, at this very spot, in Honduras, Central America. And, somehow, miraculously, Mari and I had faced its fury head on and survived. The world had something different in store for us. Something bigger.

I cranked over the engine and drove. Mitch had pummeled Honduras, and as we crept through the country, the devastation was everywhere. Entire stretches of highway ripped up and strewn about like tinker toys. Mud and water cascaded down cliffs and mountains, forming waterfalls of muck that spewed across the broken asphalt. Bulldozers were everywhere, scooping up mud and boulders and trees and other debris from the roads. Men with axes worked quickly, chopping up fallen trees and hauling the wood away with burros and carts, their faces stern and determined, pushing back against mother nature. The drizzle finally stopped, ran out of ammunition. Mari and I were exhausted. We just wanted to get home. To Nicaragua.

The truck began to vibrate, which meant I had to stop and release the fuel injectors, which were constantly getting clogged. A semi driver had taught me how to open them with my crescent wrench and bleed them of any air, a chore I'd been doing regularly for the past week. I took the opportunity to inspect our rig as a whole. The trailer had been hanging tough ever since its sixth or seventh weld job. Even the new tires seemed to be holding their own. Moving the bulk of the boxes inside the camper had helped, easing the strain on the springs and brackets. Although that also made the camper virtually useless, as it was nearly impossible to walk around inside, just a narrow passage to the bed. We hadn't showered in over a week and were eating all our meals from roadside stands where we also got our news. And the news coming out wasn't good. Hurricane Mitch had put the same beatdown of Honduras on Nicaragua. In particular, the northern mountain region where Mari's parents lived.

We picked our way along the Pan American Highway, avoiding asphalt washouts and piles of rubble, as we followed the path of semi-trucks and commercial vehicles, all traveling south through Central America. But our little caravan came to a crawl as we approached the town of Choluteca. A somberness was in the air as we watched hundreds of people walking along the muddy roads. Their faces were ashen and hollow, as if returning from war. A man placed his hand on Mari's window and pleaded for money, his eyes wide and sunk in. Death eyes. As she searched for change, the man turned and walked away, leaving a muddy imprint on the glass.

Moments later, Mari said, "*¡Ay, Dios mío!*" as we drove past rows of bright yellow bags scattered along the road. But not just any bags. Body bags. Just beyond, groups of men dug furiously down into the mud, some waist deep, others up to their chests. The end of a shovel or a hand continuously popping up from the muck and flinging mud to the side, as they searched for bodies— loved ones—to fill more yellow bags.

There were deeper pits, too—ten, maybe fifteen feet deep—where houses used to stand. Families worked together, climbing down ladders into the pits and pulling up muddy TVs, lamps, and treasured family mementos. Entire houses swallowed up by the mud, leaving but a few broken orange roof tiles peeking up through the sludge.

So much rain dumped on Choluteca that the Choluteca River changed course and flowed straight through town, flooding everything in its path and depositing a thick layer of mud. Over ten feet in some areas.

Our caravan inched along through the catastrophic scene, a column moving through the war front. A cry rang out, piercing the stale air, a wail like none I'd ever heard. It was the cry of sorrow. A child's cry. Death was all around us, and as the humidity cranked up, so too was the stench, as there was no escape from the smell of decomposition, which clung to your clothes and your skin. Then came the flies, hordes of flies, all buzzing about our heads and ears. We tried rolling up our windows, but without air conditioning, the heat became too much. I felt helpless watching as tears fell from Mari's eyes. It was all so heart wrenching. All so unbearable.

Desperate to flee the scene, we arrived at the Choluteca Bridge near the edge of town. Or, rather, where the Choluteca Bridge once stood, as the 1,500-foot bridge had been completely destroyed—washed away like a sandcastle on the beach. We got out of the truck and surveyed the wreckage. Jagged spires of rebar were all that remained, an iron exoskeleton poking out from the rubble. There was no *desvío* here. No bulldozers clearing a path. No way over or around the problem. Resilience and ingenuity had met their match.

We learned from other travelers that the northbound bridge was demolished as well, making it impossible to drive to the Nicaragua border. We'd reached the end of the road, both literally and figuratively.

"Fuck! Fuck, Fuck, Fuck!" I screamed, my words fading into the river and gap that separated us from our path forward. Mari paced nervously around the truck, worried about her family. She needed to get home. *We* needed to get home. It was time to stop bitching and whining about our situation and do something about it. I wrapped my arms around Mari and squeezed. "Don't worry, we'll find a way home."

Chapter 30

I didn't see Jen that weekend, or the weekend after. It was as if my words had spooked her, broken some silent code that forbid us from expressing our feelings, a code I developed to keep the world at arm's length. Until I met Jen. I tried working within its parameters, diving in and out of my emotions whenever I saw her. Whenever I touched her. But that desire ebbed and flowed, crashing over me like a tidal wave when I had to have her, when that overpowering desire had to be satiated. But as quickly as it rushed in, it would pull back, a constant give and take. All in and all out.

This dynamic had been playing out for years, and Jen had adapted to its rules. Now, she wanted separation, wanted the ebb. Our roles reversed. I tried playing it cool, shaking off my anxiety and burying my pain. But it's difficult to turn away from love, especially a love that has been building over the years. But Jen remained elusive. Perpetually busy. Just as I had been with her.

My San Diego friends had either graduated or dropped out by the time my senior year rolled around, so I rented a room in a large house on the edge of town. About a month in, I discovered my downstairs roommate, Carol, was a witch. And no, she wasn't just mean and nasty, although that certainly was true. She was an actual, real-life, practicing witch—who performed spells, created potions, and did other freaky shit. But, according to Carol, we had nothing to worry about, as she was a 'white' witch, whatever the fuck that meant.

Now, Carol was dating Billie, a sweet kid from the Midwest. They fought like cats and dogs. Or, rather, witches and warlocks. Epic fights that went on all hours of the night. Some ending only when the cops came banging on the door with their flashlights. One of them would occasionally disappear, hauled off by the cops, only to return a day or two later to resume the fight. Inseparable love birds.

Down the hall was Jenny, a hippie, who painted murals on the walls whenever she wasn't sketching in her notebook. Sweet and a little odd, she snuck into my room one drunken night. Other strange characters lived there, as well, but I mostly tried to keep to myself. But when Carol rented out the attic to a group of migrant farm workers, I lost my shit. She threatened me with a whole host of hexes, voodoo, and other nonsense. And when that didn't work, dragged poor Billie into the fray. I told them to fuckoff, and if they weren't careful, I'd be whipping up some of my own potions.

Needless to say, my senior year was definitely not working out as planned. I did, finally, meet up with Jen. But our 'friendship' had changed. The spark, the electricity, the attraction she felt for me, had dimmed. I didn't want to admit it, but deep down, I knew it was true.

"Pitcher?" I asked.

"Sure," she smiled. I could have sworn I saw that old glow. Who knows, maybe things could work out. Funny how our brain plays tricks in order to avoid pain.

"So," she said, "how's your senior year of college going?"

I thought about my creepy house for a moment: Billie and 'white witch' Carol, Jenny the hippy, and all the dudes in the attic. "Umm…great," I replied. "How about yours?"

Her eyes lit up as she told me about her cool, new roommates and all the fun things she'd been up to. It felt like a slow, agonizing death listening to how happy she was. While she was out in the world thriving, I was descending into my crypt.

"So, I have to tell you something…"

"What?" I asked nervously, waiting for the final nail to be driven into my coffin.

"You're not going to like it…"

"Aw, fuck, just say it!" It was the moment I'd been dreading. The final shovel of dirt atop my head. My breathing slowed, waiting for life to entomb me.

"I…I…"

"Just spit it out, for God's sake!"

"I'm joining a sorority."

Now, from the nuclear bomb I'd been expecting, of Jen kicking me to the curb completely, you'd think I'd be happy with this minor bit of news. But it hurt just the same. I had some deep-seated (perhaps misplaced) hatred toward fraternities and sororities, believing they represented everything I was not. Conforming and pretentious. And Jen held these same opinions, or so I thought. Hell, we met at a GDI meeting. GDI standing for God Damn Independence…from sororities and fraternities.

"Well, aren't you going to say anything?"

"You do realize all the shit they're going to put you through, right? Why would you want to go through that? You're a senior! You sure you want to do this?"

"Yes, I already pledged."

I didn't get it. It was like Jen was trying to cram everything into her senior year. A lifetime of experiences rolled into two semesters.

We moved onto a country western bar: Jen's pick. She put on her cowboy hat, the same hat she'd worn the night we met. Honky-tonk music swallowed the room. I felt like a fish out of water, while Jen fit right in. She grabbed my hand and let me out to the dance floor.

I tried doing the two-step but felt awkward and didn't know the moves. And when a guy with fancy boots and a big metal belt buckle asked Jen to dance, I didn't even put up a fuss. The music was so loud, we couldn't hear each other talk. So, after only thirty minutes, we left. Jen asked if I wanted to come over for a while. I felt my heart racing, thinking that maybe we could salvage the night. Salvage *us*. Pulling up to her house, I thought about all the times we'd laid together in bed, laughing and content. I yearned for that once more.

"Hold on, I'll be right back," she said, rushing out of the car. Confused, I followed her trail. She jogged up the street about fifty yards and leaped into some guy's arms. He hugged her and spun her around. I couldn't move. I was paralyzed, frozen in place. Jen was animated, smiling, a smile reserved for me. She looked back to the car, and realizing she was still in view, moved toward a row of hedges. From the shadows, I could no longer make out her face. But it didn't matter anymore. I didn't wait for Jen to return, just opened the door and slipped away. Faded into the chilly night.

Life continued to suck in the haunted house and by the time graduation rolled around, all I wanted was to get home to San Diego. I'd been working nonstop on an old, broken-down Karmann Ghia I bought for $200, and it was finally ready to drive. So, I opted to skip the graduation ceremony and hit the road. I didn't need to walk across a stage to validate all the hard work I'd put in.

"Congratulations, Mr. Businessman," said Jen. "I'm sure you'll be taking over the world in no time at all."

"Congratulations to you, too. Graduating a year early…very impressive."

"Well, that's what can happen when you actually study. Not all of us can just wing it."

"Ha! I cracked a few books here and there. But, hey, I should be going. God only knows how far the Ghia's going to make it before conking out. Enjoy your graduation."

I turned to leave, but Jen grabbed my arm and pulled me back. "Hey," she said, sliding her palms across my cheeks, "this isn't forever."

But I knew it was. And with every second I remained in her grasp; my heart was ripping further apart. I was in danger of bleeding out right there on Nord Avenue. But I didn't care. I pulled Jen in close and put my lips on hers. The blood came rushing back, along with all the raw animal attraction from before. Whoosh! Whoosh! Whoosh! I kissed her with my tongue and my lungs and my ribs. Kissed her with everything I had. Kissed her with that cocky, king-of-the-world attitude I'd misplaced over the past year. And she responded, kissing me with the same passion as the night we first made love.

And in that moment, all was right in the world.

Perfect harmony.

Zen.

Chapter 31

We drove back into town and parked the truck. Mud clung to everything: the horses and cows, the trees, the buildings (those still standing), even the people…Arms and legs, faces, entire bodies—all coated in a layer of grayish mud. And with the mud came despair, thick and heavy, and clinging to the rotting air, as we meandered through the apocalyptic scene.

"We need to find someplace to stash the truck," I told Mari in a low voice. "Someplace where it'll be safe for a while…Perhaps a long while." A boy reached out his hand and asked for some change, his fingers caked with mud. Mari handed him a dollar, and he ran off, disappeared into the gray camouflage landscape.

Entire neighborhoods lay destroyed, houses ripped clean off their foundations. Families obliterated, killed, washed clean away by the river. Body bags were everywhere, too many to count. The smell of death returned, seeping into our pores, as the people continued to dig. And dig and dig and dig. Shovels flying. Searching…for daughters and sons; mothers and fathers; friends and lovers. Searching…for something. Anything. Searching…for a life that would never be.

"Let's head over there," I said, pointing to a house on the far side of town, which, because of its elevation, had been spared. Mari just stared at a group of children, naked and digging in the mud with sticks. They were up to their knees in the muck and working at a frantic pace. Searching, perhaps, for their mother or sister. I grabbed her hand and pulled her away. Walking to the other side of town, we passed more body bags, the bright yellow canvases dotted with black flies buzzing about. I looked away, trying to avoid such an up-close view of death and decay. But my eyes kept returning to the scene, workers shoving bloated arms and legs into the bags. But it was the zipper that struck me most, that somber tone as it zipped shut, so melancholic and final, like a bow strumming a cello.

"What are you going to do?" Mari asked as we hurried up the hill and approached the house.

"I'm not sure," I replied, straightening my hair and attempting to look nonthreatening. Or as non-threatening as a person can, that's just driven through the eye of a hurricane. I knocked on the door and waited. Moments later, a woman came to the door.

"*Buenas. Yo soy Kevin, y esa es mi esposa, Maribell*," I told her, then quickly explained our predicament which was that all the roads and bridges leading to Nicaragua had been destroyed. And that we needed to continue on by foot in order to check on Mari's family and see if they were still alive. But we needed somewhere to stash our truck, camper, and trailer. I pointed to a strip of land on the side of her house. "Can I rent that area from you? Just until we can make it back, after they've repaired the roads and bridges. Please, we have nowhere else to turn."

"*Oh si, si...está bien. Y no hay que pagar*—Yes, yes, it fine," she said. "And you don't have to pay." She told us her name was Elena, then asked if we were hungry. I felt an instant relief, a burden lifting from my shoulders. We raced back to the truck, maneuvered it through town and up the hill. The tires spun and kicked up mud as I guided it next to the house. Elena insisted we come inside for a glass of mango juice and a slice of warm banana bread before we set off. As we ate, she told us about the night the Choluteca River came rushing through town, destroying everything in its wake. She said that it came so fast, and with such ferocity, there was no chance to escape. Friends who she'd known her entire life had vanished in an instant.

Mari and I packed one backpack each with clothes and a few supplies, then locked up the Beast, the camper, and the trailer as tight as possible. Elena gave us a bag of pastries, then hugged us tightly. We thanked her profusely before setting off on an unknown journey.

We made our way back to the Choluteca River, where a makeshift ladder had been propped up against the demolished bridge. Made of freshly cut branches and sticks and tied together with reeds and various pieces of rope, the ladder, descending forty feet to the riverbank below, inspired little confidence.

One man held the top of the ladder, and another the bottom, as people scaled down the rickety contraption. When it was my turn, I eased my way onto the ladder, hoping to show Mari how safe it was. But then it wobbled and rocked back and forth under my weight. I closed my eyes and waited for it to snap, bracing myself for the fall. But somehow the flimsy wood held. I wanted to race down the death trap but knew that moving too quickly would only make it worse. So, I climbed down slowly, one skinny rung at a time, as the wood bowed and stretched like some evil accordion. After making it down, I stared up at Mari. Her eyes were wide with fear. "It's not that bad!" I screamed up, lying through my teeth. Mari made it down without incident and we found a small boat ferrying people to the other side of the river for twenty Lempiras— roughly two dollars. We held on tight as the boat zipped across the river, sending spray in all directions. The cold water felt good on our skin, a welcome relief from the sweltering heat. And as we neared the far side of the river, the grisly smell of death ebbed.

After hiking up the steep, muddy embankment, we came to a stretch of freeway that was completely busted-up and twisted like a rope of taffy. But we just kicked the mud off our shoes and trudged on, sidestepping through rubble for the next four kilometers, until the asphalt became smooth once more. There, a taxi waited to shuttle people up and down the road for a fee. But the asphalt was only smooth for five kilometers, before it broke up again. We hiked for several more kilometers, crisscrossing through mud, fallen rocks, and giant boulders. A steady stream of travelers was on the road, all moving south, in unison, to unknown destinations. People began selling food and drinks to the weary travelers, entrepreneurialism at its finest. We hitched rides on the short stretches of highway that still existed, hopscotching our way across Honduras.

We spent our first night on the upstairs patio floor of a restaurant, the gracious owner providing us with pillows and blankets. We spent the following nights in other strangers' homes, shopkeepers and fellow pilgrims who'd recently made it home. We ate our meals at makeshift restaurants that sprouted up like weeds along the busted-up Pan American Highway.

Then, finally, after yet another long and grueling trek over a steep mountain pass, in sauna-like conditions, we spotted the border. The Nicaraguan border. "Yes! Yes! Yes!" I screamed, pumping my fist in the air. A smile spread across Mari's face, the first I'd seen in days, as we stepped into high gear.

Approaching the guard shack, I knew something was wrong. "*¿Dónde está la gente?*" Mari asked, as we neared the infamous yellow pole. There were no guards, no agents, no women selling tamales or vendors hawking their trinkets. No vehicles. No tourists or travelers. The border had been abandoned. I poked around some, looking inside the guard shack, and knocking on doors. But there wasn't another living soul around.

"What do we do?" Mari asked. I just shrugged and walked across the border. The first one we hadn't had to bribe our way into since Mexico. *¡Bienvenidos a Nicaragua!*

Another twenty-mile hike awaited us on the other side, traversing down the Amerrisque Mountains from El Espino to Somoto. We hitched a few rides, but Nicaragua's infrastructure was as decimated as Honduras. From Somoto, we caught a bus, which ate up a decent chunk of real estate. But eventually the road ran out, and we had to walk, our legs sore and our faces red. I sensed Mari's unease as we came to the turnoff for Pueblo Nuevo, the town where her parents lived. An eight-mile dirt road was all that stood between us and home. Mari took off at a brisk pace, almost a jog, as I ran to catch up, my thumb permanently out, hoping to catch a ride.

We'd only gone a few hundred feet when a truck pulled over. We hopped in the bed, where no less than ten other people were all squished together, clutching their backpacks to their chests. Wind whipped our faces as we bounced up and down, solemn expressions on us all. They dropped us off near the park and the church, the center of Central American towns. It was only four blocks to Mari's home, and we ran the entire way.

A scream rang out as we burst through the front door, followed by a series of people rushing toward us: Mari's mother (Albertina), her sister (Johana) and her three brothers (Noe, Eddie, and David). We dropped our backpacks on the floor and fell into their embrace, thankful they had all survived Hurricane Mitch. After several lengthy, powerful hugs, Mari and I sank into a pair of rocking chairs and exhaled. We were exhausted, yet relieved. I looked around, noticing that even the house had survived Mitch's onslaught.

Albertina cooked up some *gallo pinto* (beans and rice) and boiled chicken. We devoured it all, then crawled into bed and fell into a deep sleep. Hours later, I was awoken by the sound of rain dripping overhead. It seemed we just couldn't escape it. Mist accumulated on the edges of the clay tiles. When they became too saturated, the water dripped down. The first drop landed on my forehead, the second on my nose. I looked questioningly at Mari, but she was fast asleep. I turned my head sideways and tried to ignore it, but the water dripped onto my cheek. I pulled the sheet over my head, using it as a shield, but the heat became too much, so I ripped it away.

"Mari…" I whispered. But she didn't move. "Mari…" I repeated, louder. But she wouldn't budge—perhaps accustomed to a light spritzing while she slept. But for me, it was a different matter. I tossed and turned for hours as a steady mist coated my face. And when I finally did nod off, too exhausted to care anymore, I slept for two days straight. The sleep of the dead.

After arising from our crypts, Mari and I walked around Pueblo Nuevo and survey the damage, starting with her own house. The rain and ensuing runoff had washed away Albertina's back patio, where she cooked meals on an adobe stove. But it fared well compared to other houses which had been demolished. Overall, though, the damage was minimal when compared to the overwhelming destruction of Choluteca. However, Pueblo Nuevo was without electricity or running water, and would be for months, as Mitch had ripped out most of the electrical poles and water pipes. Yet the town and its people, including Mari's family, seemed upbeat and determined. They'd lived through adversity and hardship before. Mitch was just one more obstacle to overcome.

We got our water from a neighbor's well, bathing minimally, and used candles to light the night. Food was plentiful, as we were surrounded by farms. And we got our news from a battery-powered radio that Mari's father, Gabino, listened to throughout the day—our sole link to the outside world. Hurricane Mitch, we learned, was the deadliest hurricane to hit the Atlantic since 1780, killing over 22,000 people, destroying 50,000 homes, wiping out 70% of Honduras and Nicaragua's roads and bridges, and leaving millions homeless. Mitch dumped over 75 inches of rain atop Central America. And, incredibly, Mari and I had driven straight through that fucker!

Life settled in nicely over the next two months, as we learned to relax and enjoy life at a slower pace. We felt safe in Pueblo Nuevo. We had a home and people that loved us. Our only worry, what to make for lunch and dinner. No, we couldn't start a new business, as the economy had been decimated, but that could wait. And I was eager for the roads to be rebuilt so that I could go back for our truck and camper.

One day, without warning, the lights came on, followed by what seemed like the entire town racing into the streets to hoot and holler. A few days later, running water was restored. Soon, news arrived that a series of *desvíos* (detours) and temporary bridges had been constructed between Honduras and Nicaragua, allowing us to return to Choluteca.

We set out the next day, catching a bus to the El Espino border. The same abandoned border we crossed months earlier. Only this time, it was bustling, full of vehicles and people. After reaching the front of the line, the agent thumbed through our passports. "Where's your entry stamp?" he demanded.

"Our what?"

"Your entry stamp to enter Nicaragua."

I gave him a brief rundown, a synopsis of our journey, and finding the Nicaraguan border completely abandoned.

"Well, you must have an entry stamp. Period."

"Yes, I understand that," I said in my calmest voice. "But like I said, you guys were nowhere to be found when I was crossing the border. Because of Hurricane Mitch…You know…the hurricane that wiped out half your country." Mari grabbed my arm, hoping to prevent me from lashing out. "You realize, don't you, there was nobody here to stamp our passports?"

"Well then, you shouldn't have crossed."

"Oh, my God, are you fucking serious?" I said, switching to English. "Look, man, we had to get to Pueblo Nuevo to check on her family and you guys had bailed. That's on you, not us." The heat rose on my neck as we stood there in the scorching sun.

"Well, you'll need to pay a fine."

My head morphed into a volcano, steam sizzling off my scalp. "Now, listen here!" I bellowed. "I am an American Diplomat. Do I need to talk to your boss?"

¡Bienvenidos a Honduras!

Choluteca was a frenzy of activity, with people hard at work rebuilding the town. The sound of hammers banging and saws buzzing. We had a hard time locating Elena's house as so much had changed. The city of mud was no more. We eventually spotted the truck and camper, and to our relief, they looked exactly as we had left them. Even the trailer—the bane of my existence—was sitting peacefully in a meadow of grass.

"*¿Hola Elena, cómo esta todo?*" Mari asked. Elena rushed inside for another round of juice and pastries.

"Elena, muchas gracias por todo," I said, holding out some cash. But she refused to take it. So, while she hugged Mari, I slipped a hundred-dollar bill under my saucer. Elena truly was our guardian angel.

Chapter 32

Elena's neighbor helped us jump the Beast, and soon we were back on the road, the familiarity set in immediately as we motored south. It felt good to be finishing what we'd started. We'd been through the bowels of hell on this journey and wanted to end it on a positive note. The agents at the Nicaraguan border had other ideas, pointing to our TRANSPORTISTA sticker and telling us we had to go to Managua and pay taxes on the truck and trailer and any goods we were importing.

Before I unloaded my litany of grievances or delve into my 'I'm a diplomat' speech, an agent, who looked all of twelve, opened the door and began climbing inside the truck next to Mari. "Hey, wait a minute, what's he doing?" The other agent, perhaps his father, told us he would need to accompany us to Managua to make sure we didn't unload anything. "Unload anything? What are you talking about? All we have are personal items. I told you; we're moving to Nicaragua to live full time." My diplomat angle failed, along with every other story I tried to concoct. Bottom line: this kid was coming with us, like it or not. God forbid, we escape the taxman on all our valuable loot—the trailer of crap and the thousand pounds of books.

Turns out, our junior agent had family in Pueblo Nuevo, and since it was almost evening, we convinced him to let us spend the night there and go to Managua in the morning. After dropping him at his family's house, we sped to Mari's home and set about unpacking the trailer and camper. It was a tedious task, made easier by an endless supply of brothers and sisters and children from the neighborhood, all working in tandem to offload our 'stuff.' Once that phase was complete, a mechanic broke the welds on the tiedowns attaching the camper to the Beast, cranked up the four jacks in the corners of the camper, and lifted it off the bed, just enough so that I could drive the truck out from under it.

We set off for Managua at the crack of dawn. A family of chickens scurried about under the camper which rested peacefully on the side of the house. I should have left the trailer there too; I thought as we drove by. But our paperwork specifically listed it, and I didn't want to run afoul in Nicaragua right out of the gate. Even if I was an important diplomat. Besides, what's another hundred miles?

Three hours later, we pulled into the *Administración de Aduana, Managua*—Customs, also known as the most confusing place on Earth. They directed us from one window to the next, and one office to the next. Each person passing us off, unaware of the steps we needed to take or where we needed to go. I stepped outside for a moment before I lost my shit. Managua was sweltering. A man was sitting in a small outdoor stand drinking a Victoria beer. The bottle glistening in the sun. My jowls puffed up. I hadn't thought about booze in a long time. But I could taste that cold beer on my tongue. I hurried back into the building. Much safer inside *Aduana* hell. Mari found me and directed me to the correct office, where an older lady wearing far too much makeup told us we needed to leave our truck and trailer in a storage facility while our paperwork was completed. "And how long will that take?" I asked.

She didn't look up, just continued stamping documents like an automaton. "A month, maybe two."

The green beer bottle flashed before my eyes. The big V in Victoria. So prominent and regal. V, the Roman numeral for five. Five, the exact number of beers I would drink in the first five minutes if given the chance. I needed to extricate myself from this nightmare before I sprinted through the *Adminstración de Aduana* screaming bloody fucking murder.

The bus ride to Pueblo Nuevo was long and bumpy and crammed with people. I put my forehead on the vinyl seat in front of me and closed my eyes, bathing in my sweat and the pool that was growing around my face. It would take two-and-a-half months to process our paperwork, and only then because I made bi-monthly trips to bitch and moan and raise a stink to anybody that cared to listen, which were few. Toward the end, I brought a foldup chair and a newspaper and parked myself in the lobby for the day, waiting for somebody to release our truck.

They eventually grew tired of the smug gringo and presented us with a bill: $1200 for the truck and $500 for the trailer, import fees. To add insult to injury, they tacked on $300 in storage fees. Naturally, I was out for blood and demanded to speak to the *Gerente General*—head of Nicaraguan Customs. Hours later, when it was clear I was never leaving, a pretty lady came out and led me up a set of stairs to a large, ornate office in the back corner of the building. A fat man with a thick mustache was reclining in an oversized leather chair, smoking a foot-long cigar and flicking ashes half in, half out of a decorative wood ashtray. He glanced up, then poured himself a glass of Johnny Walker Black. *Shit! I knew I should've worn my polo shirt.* I looked down at my sweaty Quicksilver tank top and shorts while he swigged his whiskey and puffed his cigar. "What the hell do you want?" he finally blurted out. Our conversation didn't go very well. In fact, by the time I slunk out of his office, I was just thankful he hadn't raised our tariffs even higher.

I paid the $1200 for the truck, and the additional $300 for holding it hostage. But no way in hell was I paying one red cent for that fucking trailer! And as I drove the Beast off the lot, I pulled up nice and close to that piece-of-shit coffin and spit a fat loogie on it. They could have it!

Life in Pueblo Nuevo was slow and serene. Cattle rustled from one plot of grass to another. Peppers, onions, and corn shooting up through rich soil. Neighbors chatting with their neighbors. Children shooting marbles or rolling tires along cobblestone streets. Smiles and laughter everywhere. When Mari and I weren't chopping firewood, or napping, or picking up fruits and vegetables and other supplies from the outdoor market, I laid in a hammock and read, taking advantage of my cherished repository of books. But every month, when the lure of the Pacific Ocean became too strong, I grabbed my surfboard and headed west, searching for breaks along the northern coast of Nicaragua. Magellan in board shorts.

Returning from a weeklong trip to the ocean, I checked out a small strip of land that Albertina and Gabino owned just up the way from their house. It was on a slope and cut at a strange angle, with a road in the front, and a drop— perhaps forty feet down into a creek—in the rear. The land was dense with weeds, thorny bushes, and other vegetation rising ten feet in the air. A massive Guanacaste tree sprouted up from the creek below, spreading its giant branches over the strip of land. It was a beautiful setting for a house.

Gabino said it was impossible to build a house there, because of the slope and narrowness of the land. But every time I walked by it; or lay in bed with water dripping on my face—I imagined us living there, in our very own house. And one day, I snatched the machete off the woodpile, ran up the hill, and began whacking away at the brush. The blade flew about in a wild flurry as I carved a small channel into the thicket. Hours later, I sat in the dirt, sweaty and dejected. My arms, like boiled noodles, hung limp by my sides. I was exhausted and had barely made a dent in the little jungle.

But early the next morning, I was right back at it, swinging the blade with wild abandon, muscles throbbing. Thwack! Thwack! Thwack! Wiping away sweat, I noticed a few of the neighbors gathering, watching the madman at work. But I didn't have time for that. I had a jungle to clear. Yet the jungle had its own agenda: striking back at my aggression. And each time I whacked at a branch or limb or shrub, they whacked me right back. By day's end, not only was I covered in cuts and bruises, but I'd only cleared a tiny section of land. At this rate, I'd be clearing the land for months, maybe even years.

Gabino took pity on me the next day and showed me how to sharpen the blade. Amazing how much more you can cut with a honed piece of metal. But my arms were heavy, and I was running out of steam, and wondering what the point was anyway, since Gabino had told me the slope was too steep to build a house. By midday, I was dreaming about my hammock and a good book, when a couple of boys from the neighborhood appeared, each carrying a machete. Then, without a word, they entered a patch of jungle and hacked away. Minutes later, Mari's brother, David, arrived with two friends. Soon, my mini jungle was being decimated by ten-year-old boys swinging machetes a million times better that me.

By the following day, half the neighborhood kids were hard at work—girls included—mowing down the plot of land. I retired from my position as lead machete wielder, shifting more into a supervisory capacity. I paid my crew in popsicles, pastries, and soda over the next three days—which was all the time it took for them to clear the land. The kids never asked for anything in return for all their hard work. They just wanted to help the crazy gringo. I gave them all cash anyway, as they'd clearly earned it. They ran off, yipping and hollering, their infectious smiles warming my heart.

The steep slope Gabino had warned about was even more pronounced after the land had been stripped. But I was still convinced we could build a house on it and hired workers (men this time) to level it out. It took them two solid weeks, using only shovels and wheelbarrows, to finish the job. But once they did, the impossible now seemed possible. Even Gabino agreed, a house could and would go there. Time to build a house.

The first step was building a foundation. So, I grabbed David and a couple of his buddies and drove down to the local river, about a half mile from Albertina's house. The river was more of a riverbed, covered in boulders, pebbles, and sand. We fanned out and began loading watermelon-sized boulders into the bed of the truck. At the halfway full mark, she began creaking and moaning with every new boulder piled on top. When the distance between the wheel well and the tire became less than a few inches, I waved my hand and hollered, "No más!"

Wiping sweat off my face with my dirty t-shirt, I noticed a strange vehicle speeding across the embankment. I cleared my eyes and looked closer. It was a sand-colored Humvee. Perhaps, all the heat and humidity were taking their toll, as nobody owned a Humvee in Nicaragua, let alone in Pueblo Nuevo. But just then, a second Humvee raced by, followed by a third, kicking up clouds of dirt as they flew by. What the hell! I came around the truck for a closer look, trying to make sense of it all. Following hot on the Humvee's path was a desert-camouflaged semitruck hauling a bulldozer—also camouflaged. And behind the dozer was even more Humvees and more semis, all carrying different heavy equipment. Scanning the vehicles closer, I could make out the lettering on the sides. It read: U-S-M-C.

UUUURAH, Mother Fucker!

"That's my country! That's my country!" I shouted to my ten-year-old workers, before breaking into a weird dance. Something on par to a jig. But my pride was quickly overtaken by confusion, wondering why the USMC was in Pueblo Nuevo. As I was, quite literally, in the middle of fucking nowhere. And when I say nowhere, I mean nowhere. First off, I'm in Nicaragua, a skinny isthmus connecting North America to South America. Second, I'm in the mountains—way up in the mountains—in a small farm town completely off the beaten track, even by Nicaraguan standards. Third, our old buddy Hurricane Mitch had destroyed most of the infrastructure leading in and out of this region. Fourth, the U.S. doesn't have the best track record in Nicaragua. In fact, the last time we got involved here, it led to a civil war and over 40,000 deaths. So, you could forgive my shock at seeing a United States Marine Corps convoy cruising through my hood.

The lead Humvees pulled into a section of riverbed up ahead of us. Then the entire convoy came to a halt and began offloading the dozers. "*Yo regreso-* I'll be right back," I told the boys, then set off on foot to the staging area. One

Marine was making hand signals to a bulldozer driver as I approached, while another was talking on a walkie-talkie. I walked up to a soldier in a Humvee with orange hair and freckles. "Hey, what's up, bro? What are we at war with Nicaragua or something?"

His eyes lit up, and freckles danced across his face. "Well, shoot me down," he said with a drawl. "You're American?"

"Hell, yeah, I'm American." I held out my hand. "Kevin."

He shook my hand, his grip firm and rough. "The boys here just call me Tex. But tell me something, Kevin…What in the hell are you doing in this neck of the woods?"

"Dude, I live right up the road." I pointed to the dirt road they'd just come down.

"Holy shit, I never expected to see a fellow American around these parts. You sure are a long way from home."

"Tell me about it."

He called over the other Marines, who formed a circle around me and peppered me with questions about Nicaragua and why I was there. I answered each question with one of my own, learning they had arrived in Nicaragua a few days earlier, and that their mission was to rebuild the road from Pueblo Nuevo to the Pan American Highway. They were just a small contingent of a much larger force, over 2,000 soldiers spread out across the country, rebuilding roads and bridges. I couldn't help but notice how young they were. Kids fresh out of high school. For most, it was the first time they'd been off U.S. soil.

"Well, I should get back to work. I'm building a house just up the road." They offered me spools of wire and sandbag sacks, then shook my hand and got back to work. Turns out they were loading boulders and sand from the river, too. We drove back, unloaded our boulders, and returned for more.

We loaded and unloaded boulders for a solid week, working like a pack of mules. But then reality sunk in. As much as I wanted to build the house myself, I was way out of my depth. I didn't know the first thing about building a foundation with stones and cement, let alone how to lay bricks, the principal mode of construction in Nicaragua. So, we talked to Mari's father, Gabino, who told us we should hire her uncle, *Tío Manche*, to build the house. Gabino would act as foreman, since he knew a lot about construction. And my job would be to keep a steady supply of materials on hand.

Chapter 33

I had the honor of watching the United States Marine Corps in action, grading roads, and repairing bridges along a fifteen-kilometer stretch of dirt for over a month. Their caravan rolled past Albertina's house every morning, like clockwork, as I sat on the front porch drinking coffee and eating pastries. I hooted and hollered and waved my hands each time they passed. They replied by sounding their horns and pumping their fists. I'd never felt so much pride.

With the foundation nearing completion, I got an itch for saltwater and waves. Hitting the beach, no easy feat, entailed a three-and-a-half-hour journey over rugged terrain. The first section, by far the easiest, involved a long, twisting mountain descent into a valley of tobacco, cabbage, corn, and cows. The Beast navigated easily through the turns, then showed off her power on the straightaways, as we zipped by slower cars. Coming up on a Humvee, I realized it was part of a much larger convoy; A massive contingent of jeeps, Humvees, semi-trucks and other transport vehicles, all heading west to the Port of Corinto. The Marines had completed their mission, having stitched together a good chunk of Nicaragua's infrastructure. Now, 5,000 Marines were on the move, humping gear and heading home.

But as I drove across a long, narrow bridge, I spotted thirty or forty soldiers spread out along the embankment and staring down into the gorge. Their faces reminded me of Choluteca, the city of mud, and the hollow expressions worn by its people. Something was definitely wrong. I pulled the truck over and walked to the edge of the ravine. At the bottom of the canyon lay a Humvee, flipped upside down and crumpled like an accordion. Nearby, a group of soldiers carried a body bag up the muddy hill. My heart dropped. Was it Tex? Or one of the young men from his platoon? They'd all been so excited about being in Nicaragua. Now, one of their fellow soldiers was gone, soon to be flown home with a flag draped over his coffin. This Marine, this badass, this young man, who'd had his life cut short, here, in Nicaragua, a country he barely knew. But he served his country with valor. With honor.

People talk a lot of shit about the U.S., me included. Yet whenever destruction hits, or there's a need somewhere in the world—no matter how remote or far-flung—the U.S. is there. Boots on ground. Sometimes, we get it right, and when we do, it's a beautiful thing. Hurricane Mitch was one of those times.

When I returned to Pueblo Nuevo, my job shifted from transporting sand and cement to transporting brick and cement. *Tío Munche* was a machine. I'd never seen a harder worker. And in no time at all, the house took shape. *Tío Munche* did all his work by hand, using an odd assortment of hand tools, which he carried in a burlap sack. He built scaffolding from nearby tree limbs and lumber scraps and built all his cement frames and columns with rebar and sand from the river. He mixed hundreds of bags of cement, using only a shovel, forming towering volcanos and pouring water into the center. I bought him a circular saw and power drill, but they just sat in the corner collecting dust.

Tío Munche was an imposing figure, especially by Nicaraguan standards. He was well over six feet and brawny from a life of labor. His hands were large and rough, like an old catcher's mitt. And every time I shook one, it reduced me to a little boy. Besides his weekly pay, we provided him with breakfast, lunch, and a bottle of rum each day. I also made sure he had a steady supply of sand, cement, bricks, and any other supplies he required. This kept me busy most days, roaming the countryside for brick ovens. I'd order a batch of 1,500 or 2,000 bricks, whatever they could provide, then search for another kiln. We always needed more material. No Home Depot here.

In appreciation of all his hard work, I bought *Tío Munche* two bottles of rum one Friday, instead of his usual one. Later that evening, after shoveling sand all day, I returned to the house and discovered a section of the wall had toppled over. Mari and Gabino gave me an earful. *Tío Munche* could lay brick all day in a perfect line on one bottle of rum. But give him two and the entire house might fall down. Lesson learned.

After three months, it was time to put the roof on. Gabino and I argued over the pitch and type of materials to use. We'd had other disagreements, over window and door openings and other design issues, with him erring on the structural side and me leaning toward the aesthetics. But this time was different. Neither of us were budging. Consequently, all work ground to a halt.

"Why can't we just do it my way's our freaking house!" I bitched to Mari, who was caught in the middle of a tug-of-war of wills between her father and her husband. I wanted to do things my way, the gringo way. While he preferred doing them the tried-and-true Nicaraguan way. One day, the frustration became too much. So, I climbed up on the roof and began pounding nails into some of the hardest, thickest wood I'd ever seen. As if somebody had just hiked into the jungle, chopped down a mahogany tree, and thrown it on the roof. I tried ripping through it with my circular saw, but it was no match for the thick, damp wood. I switched to a handsaw after almost losing my hand on the violent kickback. Forty minutes later, while sweating like a pig and cussing up a storm, I cut through my first board.

Gabino looked on from the porch, his burlap cowboy hat tilted to one side. Lean and weathered, with a thick white mustache and piercing dark eyes, he was a prominent person in town. Even the children showed him respect, shouting "Oy, Don Gabino," whenever they ran by. I suppose I was searching for a measure of respect, too, as I struggled atop that roof, pounding thick nails into corrugated metal. By the third day, I'd made little progress, and my hands and arms were aching. I think Gabino felt sorry for me, or perhaps I'd gained a smidgeon of respect, but we reached a truce. Work resumed on the house, with me relegated back to buyer and transporter of materials; Gabino and *Tio Munche*, architect and general contractor.

In less than a month, we had a shiny new roof, and the local carpenter had measured for doors and windows. Everything was moving along nicely, for once, and I was looking forward to picking out the tile for the floor. I was running some electrical wires back to the main panel when Mari came in. It was dusk, and her shadow crisscrossed over the dirt floor. "*Quiero hablar*," she said. Her face was taut, lines stretching across her forehead.

"What's up?" I asked, my apprehension soaring. Knowing that it's never good news when somebody says they want to 'talk.' Mari fidgeted, scraping her fingernails and shifting her weight. Even worse, she wouldn't look me in my eyes.

"What is it?" I repeated.

She finally looked up, and into my eyes, then paused a moment longer. A moment that felt like an eternity. "I want to go back to the United States," she finally said.

I was confused, trying to make sense of what she'd said, searching for an appropriate response. "I'm sorry, you want to what?" Maybe I'd heard her wrong. I mean, we were finally rounding the curve, coming into the home stretch, crossing the finish line, and every other winning horse metaphor that applied.

"Kevin, we're running out of money. I want to go back to the United States and work."

I hadn't heard her wrong, no miscommunication. She wanted to leave. I had to think fast, talk fast. I agreed, things had definitely not gone as planned. In fact, everything had gone completely and utterly to shit. But I assured her that our luck would change now that the house was nearing completion. And soon we'd be able to open a business and start making money again.

"How can we open a business right now? Nobody has any money. They're all just trying to survive."

"I know, I know, but it'll change. Once the roads are repaired, the people will start spending again. We just have to be patient."

"Be patient? Are you serious? We only have $4,000 left. If we don't leave Nicaragua now, we'll be stuck here forever. Penniless and shirtless in your big empty house with no floor!"

"Oh, stop being so melodramatic. And it's *our* house." Mari was right. Our money was dwindling, especially after paying all those border bribes, taxes on the truck, and now building the house. Our lifetime nest egg had lasted a mere seven months.

"Mari, just give me a chance. I'll start making money soon, I promise."

"You do what you want, but I'm going back." She pivoted and strode away, her shadow marching in lockstep.

Chapter 34

Mari had lived her entire life poor, Nicaraguan poor, not American poor, and viewed our nest egg slipping away, as our future slipping away. There was no way she was returning to poverty. Not after seeing all the wealth and opportunity in America. All of it just sitting there, waiting for the taking. She saw us descending, while I saw us ascending. Blasting off. Two opposing views on life. The only factual truth: Mari was leaving, and there was nothing I could do to change her mind. She was as tough as that mahogany wood I'd sawed and nailed onto the roof of our house.

So, I ran down to Albertina and Gabino's house and embraced Mari with all my might, telling her how much I loved her and that, of course, I'd go back to San Diego with her. At least…that's how it played out in my brain. My body, however, had a differing opinion.

Oh, I ran all right, just not to Mari. No, I ran to the Beast. Firing her up and revving all 6.9-liters of her burly, V-8 engine. Her roar radiated throughout Pueblo Nuevo. She was the king of the jungle. I slammed her into gear and punched the gas, fishtailing as I sped away. I blew past our big, empty house, still missing its doors and windows, then hauled ass by the riverbed. The Marines had all gone home, leaving only shadows and ghosts where their caravans once traveled.

I popped in ACDC while rounding a bend on the newly graded road. My tires, my mudders, felt glued to the compacted gravel and dirt. I didn't tap the brakes once, just kept punching down on the gas. There was no way in hell I was going back to the U.S. No fucking way! If Mari wanted to go back so badly, she could go back on her own. I mean, we'd driven thousands of miles to get here, with all the shit (and I do mean shit) we owned in the world; Through Hurricane fuckin' Mitch, for Christ's sakes! How are we supposed to chuck all that now and go back?

The Beast continued to charge, rushing down gullies and up hills, across bridges and past farms, kicking up dust as we raced along the 15-kilometer road to the highway. I wish I could say I didn't know where I was going, that I was just driving my anger out. But I knew exactly where I was headed. Just as Mitch had ripped up Central America, I, too, was on a collision course with destiny.

A final arc of dirt sprayed out, as my tires left the dirt road and connected with the smooth and freshly paved Pan American Highway. Just a few miles up the road, I saw the sign for Linda Vista. The restaurant is located right off the freeway, on the edge of a small town called Condega. The Beast glided into a parking spot as if on autopilot. She'd been a trooper, guiding us through hell and back, protecting us in our time of need.

The restaurant was nearly empty, except for a couple of farmers eating enormous bowls of stew. I found a table near the back, which had a beautiful view of the mountains in the distance.

"*¿Cómo puedo servirle?*" a young lady with dark purple lipstick asked.

I didn't hesitate, not even for a moment, all of this being preordained. "*Gran Reserva y Coca*—Rum and coke," I replied. Then I sat back and enjoyed the view, noting all the different mountain peaks as my salivary glands ground away. I must have swallowed a cup of spit by the time the waitress returned. She set the rum on the table, along with a glass, a bottle of Coca Cola, a bucket of ice with tongs, salt, and a bowl of limes.

I plopped a few ice cubes into the glass and poured in some rum, topping it with Coke and a squeeze of lime. The fizz caught my eye as I smelled the dirty mixture. Condensation rolled down the glass, reminding me of that boiling day in Managua when I saw the man drinking his beer. I remembered how I could almost taste it, then, feel it oozing through my body. Well, fantasy time was over. I put the glass to my lips, carbonation tickling my nose, my year of sobriety ticking away. I savored the moment, knowing it was fleeting, like the second before climax, when your breath is in your throat; that pause before the rollercoaster drops.

Then I tilted back the glass and drank, greedily. The rum was smooth and rich, velvety, like a bar of fine chocolate. It hit all the notes. I felt no remorse, just inhaled the joy, and waited for the buzz to kick in. I drank more, sloshing booze around my tongue, the buzz, the climax—all so beautiful. This was the feeling I craved. I had sealed my destiny. It had all just been a matter of time.

The waitress returned with a candle and a lighter. Apparently, there was a power outage. I hadn't even noticed the sun had gone down. I stared at the flame as it moved back and forth, so soothing. Down and down, I fell, tumbling along, traveling that well-worn road. Flickering flames, heartache, ghosts of old.

"Yo, what's up, Kevin?"

Looking up into the dark, I saw Vek, the man from El Socorro. "What the fuck are you doing here?"

"Just traveling, my friend." His blonde hair and orange beard looked like one long mane. "It must be fate, finding you here, drowning your sorrows next to a flame once more."

"Fate? Are you kidding me? This is fucking insane! The odds are…"

"Astronomical."

"Yes…exactly." I poured another drink. "Here, try the best rum in the world."

"Thank you." He pulled up a chair and took a swig. "Ahh, you're right, it's good stuff. So, tell me, why are you alone drinking the best rum in the world?"

"Now, that's a long, boring story. Come on, man, let's drink!" I grabbed the glass and tossed it back, the rum's velvety richness having long since faded.

"So, tell me, Kevin, where have you been since I saw you last?"

"Bro, you wouldn't believe the journey I've been on."

"You'd be surprised."

"Forget about all that. Here…take another drink. Let's party!"

Vek drank some more rum and then grinned, "Hey, chief, you never answered my question back there in El Socorro. Do you know who you are?"

"Dude, not that philosophical shit again." I studied his face and his eyes. He looked so familiar. "Hey, man, have we ever met…like before Mexico?"

Vek raked his fingers through his beard. "Who's to say, brother? Aren't we all intertwined in some way?"

"I don't know what you mean by that, but you look really familiar. Like somebody I knew a long time ago."

"Hmm, maybe we knew each other in the past. Maybe we were friends. But I'm not the same person I once was. And I suspect neither are you. But it appears you have some unfinished business here, and I need to keep moving. So, I bid you farewell."

"Aww, come on, man, don't be such a pussy. Here, drink some more rum." I held out the glass, but he pushed it aside.

"I hope you work things out, Kevin, I really do."

"Work what out? I don't need to work anything out. I just need to polish off this fucking bottle!"

"By the way, did you ever figure out what your favorite Eagles song was?"

"Favorite Eagles song? Bro, are you going to drink with me or not? I don't give a fuck about any stupid Eagles song."

"I'll see you around, chief." Vek disappeared, faded into the night, leaving me alone with my rum, my thoughts, and my flickering candle. I remember little after that, snapshots of me speeding down the road blasting Back in Black. It was almost dawn by the time I pulled into Pueblo Nuevo. I pulled over a few blocks before the house and stretched out in the cab. I felt around for a towel or something to use as a pillow, but only found a CD. I popped it in and closed my eyes. As I nodded off, the Eagles came on, singing about a Desperado. I thought about Vek for a moment, and then Mari. Maybe it was time to come to my senses.

When I woke, my head was throbbing, like it'd been split in two by Albertina's rusty axe, and my mouth tasted like an old, dirty sponge. Crawling out of the truck, I stumbled to a nearby tree. With gastric juices sloshing about and my jowls trembling, I bent over and hurled an explosion of liquid vomit. Rum gushed out of me like a geyser, along with snot and tears draining from every orifice. My body trembled and spasmed before dropping to the ground. And that's where I lay, in a puddle of my barf, snot and tears, staring up at the sky.

Sobriety: Day 1.

Chapter 35

When I finally limped back to the house, tail between my legs, I noticed the dark circles around Mari's eyes. She came close and took a deep whiff. I smelled like a distillery inside of a morgue.

"You smell like a dirty pig!"

"I'm a fuckup, what can I say…"

"You are a fuckup! And you stink! Oh my God, what's all over your clothes? That's disgusting."

"I know, I know. I'm disgusting. Slap me!"

Mari looked confused, the rings growing darker around her eyes.

"You heard me…Slap me!" I grabbed her hand and swung it toward my face. But she pulled back at the last moment.

"Come on, just slap me!" I moved closer, squeezing her wrist and flinging it toward my face.

"No!" she screamed, yanking her arm back.

"Please, I deserve to be slapped."

"No, you don't deserve that. You deserve to get better. You have a cancer inside you, and you're dying."

"I'm so sorry, Mari."

"I know…"

Mari made me a bowl of red broth filled with potatoes, cabbage, and shreds of beef. Hangover medicine. Sweat and rum oozed from my pores with every bite. I wiped my face with my t-shirt and sighed.

Life's a funny thing. No matter how fast or far we run, at some point, all roads circle back. Facing our demons is a part of the journey. But if we're smart, or lucky, or both, we will have picked up some nuggets of wisdom along the way to help us when we're lying in a pool of vomit and snot. Something from our past to guide the way: an old friend, a song, a past love…a stranger within. Something or someone to push us forward. Ever forward.

I told Mari that, of course, I'd go back to San Diego with her. There was really no doubt. But I had two stipulations: I'd never work in an office or wear a tie again. She agreed, even letting a smile slip out. I loved her so much and couldn't envision my life without her. I didn't care where we lived, or what we had, or what we did, just as long as we were together.

Lying in bed that night, I thought about the crazy ride we'd been on over the past year. About chucking everything and traveling south, only to get stuck in the middle of Hurricane Mitch. Walking through the epicenter of death, and then, months later, witnessing its rebirth. Struggling with sobriety for over a year, only to give in when shit got a little rough. Yet this was life, and the experiences that would forever bind me. These nuggets of wisdom. Like seashells collected on a seashore.

My journey continues, as do all of ours. I still haven't found answers to those Mayan questions. But you can bet your ass I'm still searching.

The rain came. Light at first but getting heavier. A drop fell on my cheek, then two. I smiled and closed my eyes.

The End